FUN *(Frightened Until Numb)*

Learning To Fly Aerobatics

By

ED COLLINS

FUN *(Frightened Until Numb)*

LEARNING TO FLY AEROBATICS

Ed Collins

Published by and copies available from:

Edgar E. Collins
1240 East 100 South 18-B
St. George, Utah 84790
Fax 1–435–673–0065
Send: $21.95 plus $3.00 shipping and handling.

ISBN :   1 - 932597 - 23 - 9

First Printing: June 2004

To Linda

DISCLAIMER

This is a book on what it is like to learn to fly aerobatics. It is intended for a general audience. It is not an instruction book on how to fly aerobatics. The reader should receive tutelage from a qualified aerobatic instructor for this. The author makes no claims, expressed, implied, or otherwise as to the effect this text might have on the reader's ability to fly aerobatics.

CONTENTS

Foreword

There is something spectacular about trying something that you've never experienced before. We've all been there—in one fashion or another—with varying outcomes. To take to the skies in a tiny two seat aerobatic airplane for the vary first time in other than straight-and-level flight can be, well, the thrill of a lifetime or for some, a frightening, even a numbing experience. To purposefully tip the world off its axis and create a kaleidoscopic view of sky and earth rapidly changing places is not a daily or desired occurrence!

Why would anyone want to do such a thing? This book does much to answer that question and many more questions about the exciting and challenging sport of aerobatics. The author's own first experiences, thoughts and sensations in learning to fly aerobatic maneuvers are described in these pages and bring the reader into the cockpit. Easily understood illustrations depict the flight path of the airplane, the placement of the controls and the dynamic forces acting on the airplane during aerobatic maneuvers.

Insight and knowledge of aerobatic flight gives the reader the ability to say, "Oh, I get it! Now I know what was done! Now I know what it was about!" Pilots and non-pilots alike will enjoy reading this book—I know I did.

Patty Wagstaff

Patty Wagstaff

Six-time member of the U.S. Aerobatic Team.

Three-time U.S. National Aerobatic Champion.

Inductee, National Aviation Hall of Fame.

Airshow Headliner and "Sword of Excellence" recipient.

Six-time recipient of the "First Lady of Aerobatics" Betty Skelton Award.

Recipient of the "Bill Barber Award for Showmanship."

1996 recipient of the "Charlie Hillard Award."

Author of *Fire and Air a Life on the Edge*.

Introduction

Aerobatics! The ultimate in flying. Some might consider it reckless, out of control gyrations across the sky. In actuality it is just the opposite. Aerobatics is the very precise placement and movement of an aircraft in an extremely small well defined block of sky. Required of the pilot are total concentration and total control of the airplane. The flight path is predetermined and the pilot follows an organized set of aerobatic figures to trace out a graded routine. Flown well, aerobatics is a joy for the pilot at the controls as well as for the spectators on the ground.

So what are these aerobatic figures and what is it like for the pilot to fly them? *It's pure FUN!* No matter what their motivation is for learning aerobatics, most pilots can't help but fall in love with the sport. After learning the basics, you will want to take the next step. The best way to do this is to join the International Aerobatic Club (IAC). The IAC will allow you to climb the ladder of difficulty as high as you want, including international competition, and you will certainly enjoy the camaraderie along the way.

You will also discover the art, athleticism, and intellect required to fly aerobatic figures. A Hammerhead for example, demands a significant understanding of flight dynamics in order to perform it correctly and safely. Inadvertent spins are always a possibility when flying aerobatics so a complete understanding of how and why they occur and how to recover from them is critical. Constant attention is necessary to keep deceivingly simple rolls from loosing altitude and loops from finishing below their starting altitude. Managing the aircraft's energy, even when going backwards in a tail-slide, is the essence of aerobatics.

Take the time to read and learn more about this exciting sport. You will be glad you did.

Michael Goulian

Michael Goulian

1995 Unlimited U.S. National Aerobatic Champion.

Three-time member U.S. National Aerobatic Team.

1992 Fond du Lac Cup Winner.

1990 Advanced U.S. National Aerobatic Champion.

Author of *Basic Aerobatics* and *Advanced Aerobatics*.

Popular in-demand Airshow Performer.

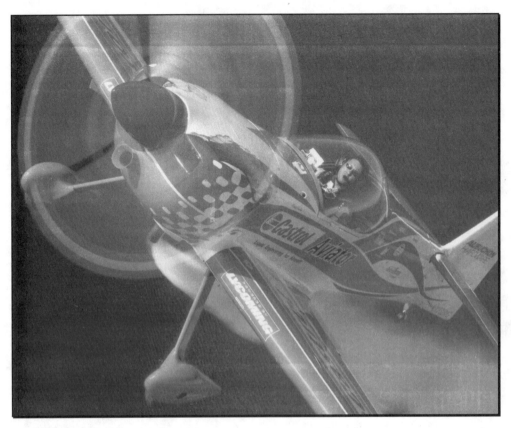

Michael Goulian in his Cap 232

Michael Goulian and author after a training flight in an Extra 200

Preview

Aerobatics is the intentional piloting of an aircraft through unusual attitudes and maneuvers. Whether performed for the purpose of entertaining an air show audience, impressing a competition judge, or for the simple entertainment of the occupants in the airplane, aerobatic flying is beautiful and exhilarating for both pilot and observer. However, without proper training, aerobatics can be deadly.

Aerobatics will subject the pilot to tremendous G loads, high speeds, and flight paths that defy both gravity and logic. The most graceful of maneuvers viewed by an audience on the ground can actually have physically grueling effects on the performing pilot.

Reading these pages you are about to be exposed to a world that very few humans have experienced. Fewer than 1% of the world's pilots have flown aerobatics. A distinctively smaller percentage has ever experienced a degree of training that would make them proficient or competitive in the sport of aerobatics. Far fewer still have ever achieved any success in competition aerobatics or on the air show circuit. The mere thought of a spin, a tumble, or even a loop is enough to scare the most veteran of commercial pilots.

The *sport,* or *"art"* as some refer to it, of aerobatics is unique. So, too, are its practitioners. Aerobatic pilots are members of a unique fraternity. An aerobatic pilot cannot find solace in a straight-and-level pilot when confronting the frustrations of minus 8 G maneuvers or complications of tail-slides. Competition pilots have established such strong bonds that they have even taken to coaching each other. Each pilot understanding that the coaching provided serves only to improve the abilities of a pilot competing for the same title.

For years, I have trained with Keith Leedom, a competition pilot from Los Angeles. We have spent hundreds of hours in the hot sun at small airports in California, Nevada, Arizona, Texas, and Oklahoma critiquing each others competition flights. Our competitive natures push each other to fly at a more precise level.

Veterans like Debbie Rihn-Harvey, a multi-time member of the USA unlimited aerobatic team, have spent countless hours training newcomers and veterans. Competitive and generous spirits such as these and many, many others have furthered aerobatics.

The uninitiated refer to aerobatic pilots as "stunt pilots." We are not. We are a disciplined group of trained pilots who choose to explore the capabilities of our aircraft. We are a group who enjoy achieving in our aircraft what may only be imagined. We do so with a dedication to the technical aspects of each maneuver we fly. We spend hours and hours of flight time refining portions of maneuvers and entire sequences of maneuvers so that we might improve our scores in a contest by a mere percentage point or so that we make one more spectator say, "wow, how was that done?"

In closing, it is important that the reader understands that the critical element to the aerobatic pilot's safety and success is training: training in aerobatic maneuvers, training in the understanding of the aircraft, and training in the understanding of the physics of flight.

Enjoy the training you are about to receive. It will allow you to enter an entire new world known as *aerobatics*!

James G. Abraham II

USA Advanced Team Member (2001)
National Advanced Points Champion (2001)
US National Advanced Championships Bronze Medal (2001)

Jim Abraham with his Extra 230

Jim…perfecting maneuvers near Las Vegas, Nevada

Preamble

Most pilots' reasons for learning aerobatics could usually fit on three fingers. They want to be safer; they want respect among peers; they want a thrill. They universally talk of improved recovery skills, to be obtained in the interest of safety, but lessons specifically geared to safety alone do not hold their interest very long—so the safety crowd is a minority. I suspect the majority learn aerobatics out of a need for respect—to get bragging rights in performing aerial maneuvers best associated with astronauts and steely-eyed missile men. The desire for respect is not readily admitted however and the reality of a few lessons soon illustrates that respect is earned; it's not so much to have experienced aerobatic flight—anyone can go for a ride—but rather achieving true mastery of the airplane in the most ridiculous of positions, that merits respect. So respect as a motive diminishes a bit in the face of the work required to earn it. Of the pilots who get past their initial aerobatic lessons, many become highly motivated for the final and lasting reason. The sport is FUN in capital letters, and becomes something of an addiction. With the author's professional credentials, I suspect he'd recognize this and look for a cure. In my professional opinion, however, he's a lost cause. Our early lessons together sparked a delightful passion for the sport that is, thankfully, incurable.

Most pilots experience a sense of freedom in the air—the ability to cross distant horizons, and defy gravity in a money-burning machine, rising above our earthly existence and so on—but aerobatic flight adds joy to that freedom, in a complex mixture of challenge, skill and fear. The thrill is incomparable to most earth-bound endeavors, with competitive gymnastics bearing the most similarity. Aerobatic maneuvers are physically demanding yes, but the biggest challenge is mental—perfect maneuvers require discipline and focus akin to the finest game of golf. Perhaps it takes another pilot to appreciate it best, but this book does much to bring understanding of aerobatic flight to the layman. Introducing pilots to aerobatic flight ranks among my favorite occupations. When a pilot learns a new maneuver, overcomes some previously held limitation, and literally blossoms up there, the rewards, for me, are many.

Ed has written kindly of me in this book—I'm grateful; but truth be spoken, learning of this nature is an individual experience and is, despite efforts of the best instructors, ultimately personal. I'm glad to have been there for the beginning.

Wow. Give a guy a few lessons, and look at him go!

Lewis Bjork

Lewis Bjork just before a training flight in the Decathlon. Notice the subtle smile.

Lewis Bjork is a Captain with Skywest Airlines and holds an ATP certificate, CFI-ME, and Instrument ratings. He has given over three thousand hours of flight instruction with aerobatics, tail wheel, and off-airport landings a specialty. He has authored two books, *Piloting for Maximum Performance*, and *Piloting at Night* along with editing the *Basic Piloting Handbook,* and co-editing the 8th edition of *Modern Airmanship.* He has flown over a 130 different types of airplane (some as test pilot) and is currently building a Pitts model 12.

Acknowledgements

Aerobatics is a demanding sport. To be competitive requires, as in any sport, generous sacrifices in time, and money as does writing about these experiences. For me these efforts would be only remotely possible without the help of family and friends. First, and foremost therefore I thank my wife Linda. Her unwavering support has been inspirational. All of the family including the children Stephen, David, Lara, and John are thanked for putting up with endless conversations about flying aerobatics, competitions and for critiquing my early fledging efforts. Instructors, friends, and coaches have been key to any progress, improvement, or knowledge attained. Among these to be thanked are Lewis Bjork, a natural born pilot if there ever was one. Greg Poe, who can precisely tumble and contort an aerobatic aircraft to create amazing figures. Michael Goulian, a champion and a gentleman who can snap roll an aircraft like no-other. Phil Knight, whose knowledge, accomplishments and experience in flying are endless and shared with enthusiasm and expertise. Alan Geringer, who some how knew exactly what I was doing in the cockpit just watching me from the ground. Jim Abraham, who flies with the deft skill of a surgeon. Bubba Vidrine, who is as entertaining on the ground as he is in the air. Also to be thanked are the many pilots with whom I have had the privilege of knowing and associating. Their encouragement and comments are appreciated more than can be expressed. In addition, special thanks and acknowledgement to Patty Wagstaff, who has made flying aerobatics an art form of beauty and precision.

Prologue

You feel the rising G-forces as you pull back on the control stick and your weight doubles and doubles again. You guide your small, one seat, brightly colored aircraft into a curved ascending path. Assured that the harness around your hips and shoulders will hold you securely, you continue tracing an upward arc in the sky while moving more and more onto your back. You find the sensations change briefly to weightlessness as you relax the backward pull on the control stick and hang from the straps, upside down, floating over the top of the arc. Gravity tugs the plane earthward. You resist by holding tightly to the control stick to carve out the completion of the circle. You are pressed hard into your seat as your weight again quadruples to 4-Gs. At precisely your starting point and speed, you release the back pressure on the control stick and return to level flight. A perfect loop. You look back at the dissipating smoke trail. Beautiful!

Welcome to the world of aerobatics. It is a place where the ultimate in flying will be experienced. There are challenges to meet here, fears to over come, skills to learn, doubts to be replaced with confidence, thrills to know. If ever you have wondered what it is like to fly with grace and expression, tracing figures across a giant canvas sky, as if your tiny airplane were the tip of a brush marking wisps of white curves and straight lines that fade with the wind against the soft blue. If ever you have stood and watched a spectacular display of flying and wondered how such precision and beauty is accomplished then you are among the many, both pilot and non-pilot alike, who wish to learn more about aerobatics. This book will take you inside the cockpit with narrative and conversations between instructor and student during aerobatic training flights. The authors own first experiences, thoughts, and sensations during these early attempts are described in such a way that it feels as if you the reader were at the controls. Discussions of what went right, what went wrong, and why for particular aerobatic figures and maneuvers are incorporated into each chapter. The dynamics of aerobatic flight are explained in simple terms and with drawings. You the reader will learn enough about aerobatics to be able to say. "Now I know how that is done." Come with me then to loop, roll, spin and fly straight down and straight up, even backwards and upside-down.

Chapter 1

The Hammerhead

The Hammerhead.

One of the most graceful and beautiful of all aerobatic figures the hammerhead is as enjoyable to fly as it is to behold. The aircraft ascends on a perfect vertical line until it can no longer continue upwards. It then pivots exactly 180 degrees and descends on the same vertical line.

1

THE HAMMERHEAD

First Attepts

"Think of it"......I said to my wife Linda as we sat across from each other at our favorite restaurant, "say this is the airplane".....and I held my fork up at eye level. "First you fly straight up...and then you fly straight down." I explained as I moved the fork around with dramatic flair. Linda's smile broadened with a touch of embarrassment as she glanced at others nearby, hoping I wouldn't add muffled engine noises to my make-believe airplane.

I had recently purchased a beautiful yellow and black Super Decathlon N1118E (Figure 1-1) after having been away from flying for several years. Over the preceding weeks I had been learning how to handle this aerobatic tail-dragger and had employed the services of Lewis Bjork, a well known local flight instructor. Today we were going to fly a maneuver called the hammerhead. What could be more exhilarating, I thought, what could be more fun, what could be easier? I wanted to share my excitement.

"Won't the airplane just fall backwards after flying straight up, how do you turn it around so quickly?" She asked, gently reaching for my fork.

"I don't know." I said motioning with my hand, "it just turns around on a dime and you fly straight back down…isn't that great?"

1-1 Super Decathlon N1118E

Just then our food arrived and my fork became an eating utensil again. The conversation shifted to other concerns and I was left flying straight down, still wondering to myself how the airplane could turn around like that. Linda's question would have to go unanswered for the time being. After lunch, I headed for the airport still wide-eyed with anticipation.

It was just a short drive to Bountiful Skypark, a small airport not far from Salt Lake City, where I was to meet my flight instructor.

Young, and in his late twenties, Lewis had a playful grin and a matching wit. Thin and long legged, he scrunched into the back of the tandem seat Decathlon folding a bit at the knees and waist. The backpack style parachute pushed him to the forward edge of the seat where he was held by the various straps of the aerobatic harness. I was a bit more comfortable in the front seat wearing a similar parachute and harness with straps pulled tightly across my hips and others over my shoulders and the ends snapping into a central locking mechanism in the front at my waist, which was then pulled down tight with a bottom strap. A secondary shoulder and waist restraint similar to a seat belt completed our packaging. Parachutes are required for aerobatic training flights in the United States and though seldom needed have been a welcome option for those who have utilized them in an emergency. The aerobatic harness held us securely in our seats yet allowed freedom of movement of our arms and legs and head for management of the controls and to look around for orientation.

Head sets in place and the intercom on I heard Lewis announce, "How do you read?"

"Loud and clear," I answered.

With check-list complete we were ready for take off. We had, in previous flights, reviewed basic flight maneuvers and various landing techniques in the Decathlon and had even done some loops. I was anxious now too finally do some real aerobatics. I felt I was getting the hang of this stick and rudder stuff and was ready for a new challenge, or so I thought.

We had talked about the hammerhead (or stall turn as some call it) during preflight. It all seemed so simple. Just establish a vertical line and when the momentum of the aircraft bleeds down push hard left rudder and control any roll or pitch with aileron and elevator. A piece of cake. How hard could that be? Precise timing was emphasized as was position and attitude of the airplane and something about not getting upside-down and on our backs in the turn around.

"Remember, exactly vertical on the pull up, check both wing tips to see that they are perpendicular on the horizon," Lewis admonished.

"OK...OK...got it," I answered.

We flew north, then along the shores of the Great Salt Lake to the practice area. It was a perfect day. Winds were light and visibility seemed endless except for a few clouds.

"Let me demonstrate the hammerhead to you," Lewis stated interrupting my distant thoughts, "just follow along with me."

The Decathlon is fitted with dual controls (Figure 1-2). Each of us had a control stick for movement of both the elevators, which are at the tail of the aircraft and the ailerons which are at the trailing edge of the wings. Pulling back on the stick caused the airplane to climb because the elevator would deflect up into the wind and the tail would be pushed down.

1-2 Dual controls allows each pilot to follow the others inputs.

Moving the stick left or right would cause the airplane to roll in the desired direction. For example, moving the stick to the left would cause the aileron on that wing to rise. The wind would push that wing down causing the plane to roll. Similarly the aileron on the right would deflect but in the opposite direction. The wind would lift the right wing aiding the roll.

The controls for the front and back pilots were connected, so any movement Lewis made with his stick caused my stick to move in the exact same way. The rudder pedals were similarly connected. Pressing a pedal would cause the nose of the airplane to move to that side. The deflected rudder at the rear of the airplane would catch the wind and swing the tail oppositely. It was easy to see and feel the control inputs of each other, but not so easy to learn just when and how much to move the controls.

Things happen fast in aerobatics and getting behind the action is a common error, as I soon discovered. On our previous flights of coordination exercises including steep climbing and descending turns, Lewis would nudge the controls this way or that to teach me proper placement. I was also getting more used to the sensation of positive G forces when pulling back aggressively on the stick. This action would plant you firmly in your seat as if a 500 pound gorilla had just sat on you.

"Ready...here we go," Lewis announced.

We dove for speed and leveled off at about 140 mph. The pull up to vertical was crisp and precise and the 4 G's caused by abruptly turning the plane skyward pressed me hard into my seat for just a couple of seconds. Looking left and right I could see both wing tips lay relatively perpendicular on the horizon as if they were perfectly balanced on a string. The nose pointed skyward. I lay on my back enjoying the 500 ft. ride upward with little sensation of movement at all. Momentarily, I felt Lewis push the left rudder pedal to the floor and then move the stick here and there as the plane quickly and exactly reversed direction. Seconds before I had been looking at a soft blue sky and billowy white clouds, now I was looking at nothing but hard brown earth. The sensation of movement returned as I starred straight down. The landscape below began looking large and then larger still. We were picking up speed rapidly. This gentle ride going up had now suddenly changed to a wide-eyed, muscle tensing, anxious dive going down. It's about time to end this thing I thought to myself as we pulled out to level flight and at our original altitude and speed. Well that was easy, I reassured myself, piece of cake, nothing to it, just like I figured, pull up, turn around, come back down…my turn.

I nervously took the controls, dove for some additional speed, leveled off and then with a deep breath yanked back on the stick.

"Vertical Ed, get vertical......both wings perpendicular on the horizon.........hold it ....No.....No......too far............OK my airplane," Lewis uncharacteristically barked.

Coming back down… after a botched hammerhead.

The airplane bobbled around and jerked a bit, like a dog at the end of a leash, and then quickly headed back earthward as if trying to escape from its tormentor. Lewis got us back straight and level again then stated, "OK your airplane, this time a little easier on the pull up and release the back pressure on the stick when you get perpendicular...try again."

Finding the vertical up line was a lot more difficult than expected. Just pulling back on the stick was not sufficient at all. Not enough pull would put us too shallow. Too much would put us on our back. Off by even a few degrees and the maneuver was ruined.

I tried again...same problems...not enough or too much pull on the stick.

The vertical line seemed to be more of an illusion to me than a reality. Sure it had to be there...someplace...I just couldn't find it. The mistakes were endless. One wing was always down, usually the left. Trying to look to the right to check both wing tips felt somehow unnatural as I tended invariably to look to the left most of the time. Occasionally I thought I had the vertical nailed only to find myself arcing backwards. Most of these first attempts ended in a sort of flat-sided, partial loop, with a flop over and a turn or something close to it at the top. Not pretty or graceful at all.

Seeing my frustrations Lewis tried one.........perfect! Darn that guy anyway, I thought to myself, I've got to show him I can do one of these. I took a firm grip on the control stick with feet pressed firmly against the rudder peddles. Throttle was set for full power allowing my left hand to be free. This must be how a cowboy feels in a saddle-bronco competition I figured. OK crank and yank to vertical then kick and whip to turn around on top. OK,... I'm ready...open the chute.

"Nice and easy Ed, we don't want to break anything, adjust the power at the time of the pivot if you need too." Lewis advised.

I relaxed some, that helped, but things were not much improved. We set up to try again. As the airplane slowed at the top of the vertical line, it seemed to have a mind of its own. It would roll and pitch at about the time full left rudder was being applied to make the turn around. I tried to make adjustments by moving the stick here and there but that just seemed to make everything worse. I wasn't coordinated well with the rudder pedals either and the plane wiggled around like a puppy's tail rather than holding a true or straight line.

I tried again…same problem…and again…different problem. Things were getting worse, not better, and the frustrations from each attempted just compounded everything.

Instructions from the back seat refocused my attention.

"This time I'll set the line and you just push left rudder when you think it's time and adjust the power and put the stick where you think it needs to go. Feel the airplane and sense what it is trying to do, stay with the action." Lewis suggested.

"OK, I can do that."

Up we went, then as the Decathlon slowed to 40mph indicated airspeed I pushed hard left rudder. We turned at the top then bobbled some before heading straight down. We had flown over an area having intersecting roads at right angles. We used these as our ground references. Tracking north along the road directly below would also be our reference going south because the hammerhead maneuver would reverse our direction. The intersecting right angle road in the east-west direction would be our reference in the pivot for the wings to track along as we changed from flying straight up to straight down.

"Where's the road Ed?" Lewis questioned.

I looked, it was strangely not directly below us as it should have been, neither was the intersection and besides that we were headed southeast, not south.

"What do you think you are doing wrong?" He added.

"Everything," I returned with an obvious sense off frustration.

"Good answer," Lewis affirmed after a long pause and then a chuckle. "This hammerhead stuff takes a lot of concentration."

Demonstrating a few more Lewis called out key points along the way and then we headed back to the airport. I felt defeated. This was supposed to be easy, like falling off a log or riding a tricycle. It felt more like juggling, patting my stomach, and line dancing all at the same time.

We landed safely, talked a bit more about the flight while putting the airplane away, and then I headed for home. It hadn't been a good afternoon.

"Well, how did it go?" Linda asked with a knowing smile.

"Uh..........not bad..........not bad."

"Straight up,… and straight down?" She said, gesturing with her hand.

"Define straight." I countered, as we both broke into laughter.

Runway in sight.

Reflections

My first attempts at the hammerhead were a lesson in humility. Simple, this maneuver is not. To learn to fly this aerobatic figure correctly I reasoned it need to be broken down into its various parts and each part studied until understood, then add the next part and so on. Practicing those basic flight coordination exercises probably wouldn't hurt either.

It was evident there was more going on with the flight dynamics than I had realized. I found that input given on the controls will, hopefully, direct the aircraft in the manner wished, however, input on the controls will often introduce something not wanted at all.

Just cranking up the speed, then yanking back on the stick to fly skyward until out of energy, and then kicking the rudder to whip around and come back down wasn't a hammerhead at all. Not even close. Its appearance was more like a badly bent paperclip, not pretty or graceful, and not much use either.

With the challenge at hand to learn the intricacies of this graceful maneuver, and the control movements necessary to make it look graceful and precise, I found myself doing a lot of reading. Many excellent pilots have written about this and other subjects concerning aerobatics. Their works are listed in the bibliography. It became apparent that I needed to learn as much as possible about the maneuver and what happens to the airplane when the control surfaces are deflected. I needed to think it through, realizing though that knowing it, and doing it, are a long way apart. Yet there was no chance of doing it without knowing it… that would be even further remote.

Things happen fast in aerobatics. Figuring it all out in real time, I reasoned, would come only with knowledge and endless hours of practice. Even then it seemed there would be occasional surprises. Things didn't happen the way I thought they would when I tried my hand at the hammerhead. I wanted to know why. Here are some of the things I have learned, then and since.

Gyroscopics

My next flight wasn't really a flight at all. I sat in the cockpit of my airplane while on the ramp and before starting the engine, looked at the propeller (Figure 1-3).

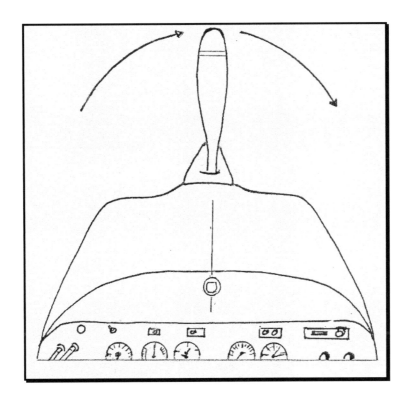

1-3 Cockpit view of Super Decathlon. From the pilots viewpoint the propeller rotates clockwise with the blades descending on the right and ascending on the left.

From my position, the propeller rotates clockwise. A rotating propeller is much like a spinning disk that resists movement from the geometric plane in which it is spinning. I could however move the propeller in pitch by moving the stick forward or backward. This would cause the nose of the aircraft to go up or to go down. I could move the propeller in yaw by pushing the rudder pedals which would cause the nose to move left or right. In making these movements the gyroscopic energy, which is present in any spinning object, is disturbed and tends to reestablish equilibrium by moving 90 degrees around the circle from the point of disturbance. (Figure 1-4)

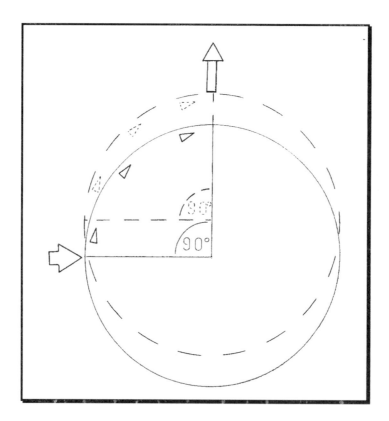

1-4 The propeller as a rotating disk. A disturbance on the left side of the rotating disk causes the gyroscopic energy to move 90 degrees around the disk in the direction of rotation. The disk wants to move up.

This movement is referred to as gyroscopic precession. It can be felt most when the aircraft is at high power and low airspeed as at the end of a vertical climb.

The propeller can be thought of as a spinning disk with top, bottom, left and right sides. Depressing the left rudder would be like bringing the left side of the disk toward me as the nose of the airplane swings to the left. Having disturbed the gyroscopic energy on the left of the circle the reaction is to seek equilibrium by moving 90 degrees in the direction of rotation. Since the propeller is rotating clockwise, 90 degrees from left is up. By pushing the left rudder pedal the nose of the airplane swings to the left, which is what is wanted, and it will also move up because of gyroscopic precession which may not necessarily be wanted. (Figure 1-5)

1-5 In an upright aircraft, depressing the left rudder pedal causes the nose of the aircraft to swing left because of air against the rudder (the tail swings to the right). The nose also moves up because of gyroscopic precession.

Pulling back on the stick of an upright airplane will cause the nose to go up. It will also cause the nose to move to the right because of gyroscopic precession. This can be thought of as pulling back on the top of the spinning disk (propeller). Having disturbed the top of the disk, the gyroscopic reaction is to reestablish equilibrium by moving 90 degrees around the circle from the disturbance. Ninety degrees from up is right. So pulling back on the stick causes the nose to go up, which is what is wanted, but gyroscopic precession also causes the nose to turn to the right which may not be wanted. (Figure 1-6 and 1-7)

Just sitting there in the cockpit, thinking, I was starting to understand some of the things I had been doing wrong in the hammerhead maneuver. This cold engine flying wasn't burning gas or putting time on the tachometer. I figured I had better sit and think some more.

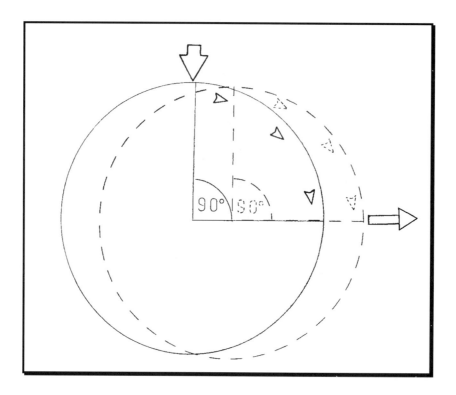

1-6 A disturbance at the top of a rotating disk causes gyroscopic energy to move 90 degrees around the disk in the direction of rotation. The disk wants to move to the right.

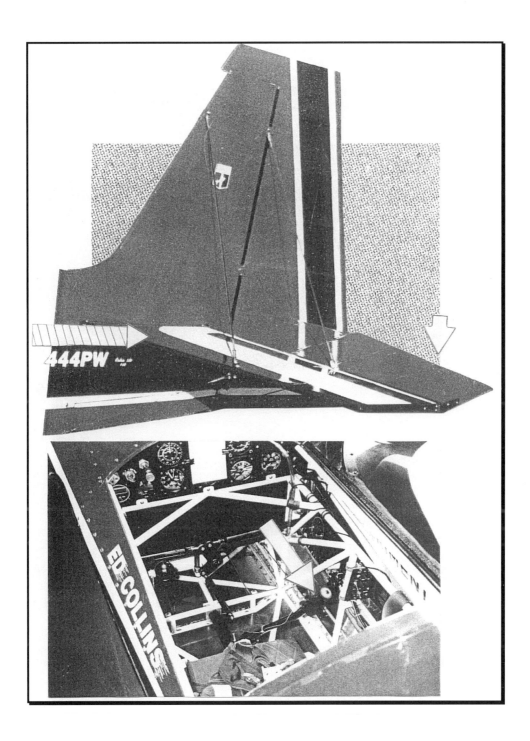

1-7 Extra 230. By pulling back on the stick the nose of an upright aircraft rises because of air flowing over the deflected elevator pushing the tail down. The nose also moves to the right because of gyroscopic precession.

I centered the stick and looked left and right at the ailerons and back over my shoulder at the elevator. Both ailerons and elevator were neutral...perfect. That should be straight and level flight or close to it I felt. Holding the stick with my right hand I pulled back as I would to initiate a vertical climb. I didn't need to move the stick far, maybe a couple of inches or so. I looked again at the ailerons. If I had pulled the stick directly back the ailerons should have remained neutral. They weren't! What's causing that, I wondered. Re-centering the stick, I watched the left aileron as I pulled back. It rose ever so slightly. Over compensating, I pulled back again as if I was lifting a barbell. The right aileron went up! "Wow, this thing is really sensitive," I exclaimed!

I sat there for awhile, moving the stick back-and-forth until I could make the full excursion from full forward to full aft stick without the ailerons moving at all. By the time I finished I was holding the stick by my thumb and two fingers. No need to grab tight and yank hard. When I tried that the ailerons deflected.   "Hmmm," I uttered as I further relaxed. This is artful finesse, like drawing a fine straight line.......bronco-riding mentality is not required.

I worked the stick forward and aft trying to program the feel of that movement. I knew it would be different in flight with air pressure on the control surfaces but the idea of feeling the movement of the stick was helpful.

Again placing the stick in the neutral position I moved it left and right trying not to cause any movement in the elevator. This was a lot more difficult. Moving the stick all the way to the left was one type of movement. Moving it to the right was another and involved different muscles. Again there was no need to act like I had a barbell in my hand but rather a fine brush to draw a perfectly straight line.

I marked the spots for full left and right aileron with tape and watched myself move the stick left and right checking to keep the elevator neutral. Drawing a straight line without curving at the ends took some practice. I tried putting both hands on the stick to see if that helped balance the muscle movements. To me it felt unnatural and reminded me of sawing a log. It did help to keep the line straight though.

What other forces act on the airplane? Pondering this question I recalled reading about various flight dynamics including "P" factor, slipstream, and torque which all seemed to be associated with a spinning propeller, added to that were uneven lift and rudder movements. A glider pilot, I suppose, would not have all these concerns about the effects of a propeller and could slip through the air focusing on lift and control deflections and the like. Personally though, I like the comfort of a little noise up front, so putting up with this spinning air foil seems therefore less of a problem.

Let's discuss each of these flight dynamics individually.

Torque

Torque is a force created by the rotating propeller. With the propeller attached to the engine, and the engine attached to the airframe, this force is resisted and in fact tries to rotate the aircraft in the opposite direction. This principle of action and reaction is referred to as Newton's first law of physics. It is most evident with sudden blasts of power. Torque on an aircraft with a huge engine and short wings, such as those seen in air races, could easily twist the aircraft opposite to the direction of propeller rotation causing it to roll suddenly should the pilot jam the throttle to the firewall. The effect of torque can also be evidenced when the aircraft is moving slowly but is at full power such as at the end of a vertical climb or any maneuver resulting in the nose pointed skyward and the airspeed slow.

"P" factor

Look again at Figure 1-3. The clockwise turning propeller blades travel down on the right and up on the left. The leading edge is of course the most forward portion of each blade. Each blade has an equal rearward twist which places the tip at approximately 45 degrees in relation to the hub (Figure 1-8).

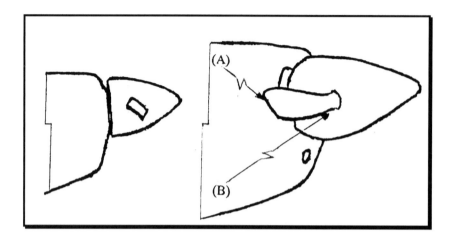

1-8 The tip of the propeller blade (A) is at approximately 45 degrees to the hub (B).

If one blade strikes the air more flatly it pulls harder on that side. Compare this to sitting as far forward as possible in a row-boat, and paddling only on the right, at the bow. Essentially the force of the paddle pushing against the water turns the boat to the left. With this in mind, picture what would happen if the down going propeller blade, the one on the right, encountered more air on that side. The force of pushing more air away from the nose on the right would turn the aircraft to the left. What could cause this? Look again at the propeller blades. If the angle of attack is increased by raising the nose of the aircraft, the down going blade encounters a larger portion of air than the up going blade. It's sort of like the down going blade is slapping at the air and the up going blade is slicing through it. This unequal force moves the nose of the airplane to the left.

Slipstream

The work of the propeller on undisturbed air creates thrust to move the airplane forward. Along with thrust, however, comes swirling air. The spinning propeller causes the air to spiral back along the fuselage of the airplane. This is called slip-stream. The twisting spiraling air has its greatest effect on the flat vertical surfaces of the airplane such as the fuselage and the vertical stabilizer. The clockwise turning propeller swirls the air around the fuselage, with the greater force being exerted along the left side. This tends to push the nose to the left much as if you had pushed lightly on the left rudder pedal. Slip stream effects are felt mostly at slow speeds and high rpm's which causes the spiral to be very tight. With increased speed the slipstream is elongated and less of the spiraling air strikes the fuselage. Look at Figure (1-9).

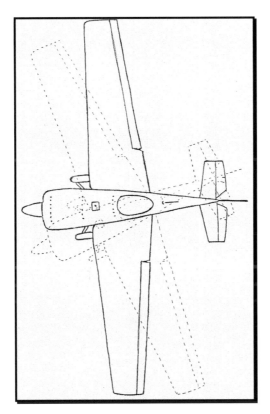

1-9 As the spiraling air moves back along the aircraft it strikes the left side of the fuselage and the vertical stabilizer. This slip-stream effect moves the nose to the left.

Understanding what the propeller is doing to effect the flight characteristics of an airplane, especially at low speed and high rpm's, helped me to better grasp what was taking place in a maneuver such as the hammerhead.

Now if I could just get the control movements down pat…I might be able to pull one of these off.

Straight and level flight

I must really be loosing it, I thought. Sitting here, trying to figure out straight-and-level flight. It's the first thing you learn to do in flight training and should be as natural as walking, you just do it without thinking about it. I looked again at both wings. They were, of course, aligned with the ground at an angle as the plane sat there on the ramp, resting back on its tail wheel, and its nose pointing upward. In the air and flying, the plane would be more level. There would be, however, the ever slightest angle of the wing against the horizon when the plane was in level flight. This angle of incidence is caused by the position in which the wings are attached to the fuselage and varies with aircraft models. Taking this into account the wings are still referred to as level with the horizon when in level flight. Keeping the wings perfectly level in flight, angle of incidence considered, would require constant checking of both wing tips against the horizon. I had come to realize that even the slightest movement of the stick could create a compounding problem if not corrected immediately. Lewis had admonished me to check both wing tips prior to the pull to vertical.

 The reason becomes clear by looking at what happens if the aircraft is not perfectly straight and perfectly level before changing the direction of flight (Figure 1-10).

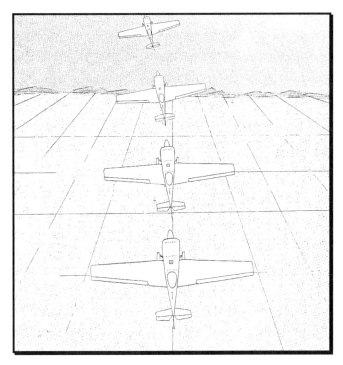

1-10 Pull to vertical with one wing low in an Extra 230. The wings must be perfectly level on the horizon before the transition to the vertical line. In this example, the aircraft is off to the left. Pushing the right rudder to regain the vertical line may help but the correction will still be noticeable.

With one wing low, by even the slightest amount, the transition from horizontal to vertical flight will not put the plane on the vertical line but rather skewed off on an ever increasing departing angle. The error becomes readily apparent. To correct it a side slip may be tried by pushing right rudder in this example to regain the vertical line. "Oops.......to far........oh no........out of energy..........this is a real mess," I could see and hear myself trying to fly those first vertical lines. Many aerobatic aircraft are equipped with sighting devices. These can be elaborate triangles of 45 and 90 degrees formed with light weight metal rods, or tubing, and attached to the wing tip (Figure 1-11). Or they can be as simple as a piece of tape on the canopy set at these angles. A sighting device probably would have helped me..........as I needed all the help I could get.

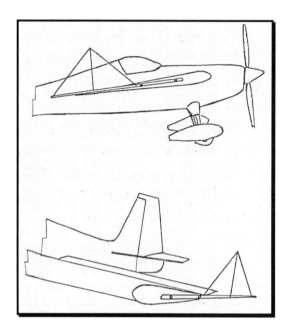

1-11 A sighting devise, such as this attached to the wing tip, is a welcome aid for setting 45 and 90 degree lines.

Uneven lift

This situation arises when the rudder is used to yaw the nose of the aircraft left or right. It is generally at low speeds as in a spin or a tight turn such as the hammerhead. It is also seen in accelerated stalls where rudder is used to snap roll the aircraft.

As the nose yaws in the direction of the applied rudder, the wing on that side moves slower and in a smaller arc being on the inside of the turn. The wing on the outside of the turn inscribes a larger arc and is moving faster and developing more lift. The outside wings greater lift rolls the plane to the inside of the turn. For example, at the top of the vertical line in the hammerhead when rudder is applied to yaw the nose from straight up to straight down.   Now let's say we are turning to the left, the left (inside) wing develops less lift than the right (outside) wing. The aircraft turns and rolls left.

Because it is rolling and turning the aircraft ends up past the vertical down line, and a bit on its back, unless adjustments are made. Also by deflecting the left rudder in this situation there will be gyroscopic effect that additionally lifts the nose past the vertical line.

Putting it all together

It was time to start the engine, and go flying. I had reviewed in my mind what I thought I needed to know to improve my ability to perform this one maneuver. I went over it all again step-by-step.

First, fly over good ground references such as roads or fields with clear right angle intersecting lines. Dive for speed and level off at 140-160mph for the Decathlon. Establish straight and level flight (Figure 1-12).

Super Decathlon. Notice that back stick raises the elevator. In flight the tail would be pushed down by the relative wind and the nose of the aircraft would rise upwards to set the vertical line. Once the vertical line is established the back pressure on the stick is released.

1-12 Hammerhead to the left, (a) straight and level flight, (b) pull to vertical, (c) hold the vertical line, (d) pivot with left rudder, control torque, slipstream, gyroscopic precession, and uneven lift with right aileron and forward stick, adjust power if needed, recover just past 135 degrees of pivot, (e) hold the vertical down line, (f) pull out of the dive.

Check both wing tips to make sure they are level and on the horizon. Next is a smooth deliberate pull to vertical. The high speed causes the gyroscopic effects to be relatively small yet P-factor will be present because of the increased angle of attack as the nose comes up. Right rudder pressure will therefore be necessary to keep the vertical line.

Quickly check both wing tips to make sure they are now perpendicular on the horizon and release back pressure on the stick.

1-13 Flying the vertical down line in a Super Decathlon. Look at both wing tips to make sure they are held perpendicular to the horizon, both on the up line and the down line.

Control pitch with elevator, roll with aileron, and yaw with rudder to hold the vertical line. An ever increasing amount of right aileron and right rudder along with forward stick pressure is needed as the plane slows on the vertical line. OK.....get ready for the turn around........hold the line........hold the line........watch the left wing for forward movement as the plane gets slower and torque effect becomes greater. Listen and feel for buffeting of the fuselage............Now...........smooth full left rudder........watch the left wingtip slice over and along the reference below.

Engine torque is trying to roll the airplane to the left, as is uneven lift. Right aileron is therefore needed in the pivot. Full left rudder at slow speed and full power will cause the nose of the aircraft to rise because of gyroscopic precession. Some forward stick is necessary to keep the nose slicing along the ground reference. The amount of right aileron and forward stick in the pivot is not always the same, is different with different aircraft, and is dependent on speed, timing, wind, and rudder movement, along with the effects of torque, slipstream, gyroscopics, and uneven lift. Reducing the power as the plane pivots may be helpful if engine and propeller effects can not otherwise be managed with stick and rudder inputs (Figure 1-13 and 1-14).

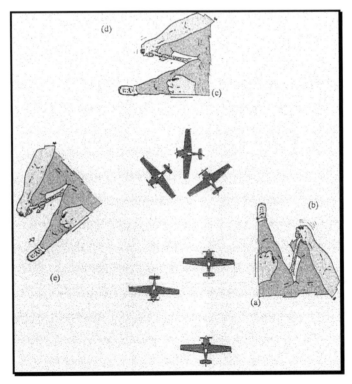

1-14 Stick and rudder positions on the pivot, (a) full left rudder, (b) right aileron then forward stick, (c) adjust power if needed, (d) adjust right aileron and forward stick as you watch the left wing track along the ground reference, (e) get ready to quickly reverse rudder just past 135 degrees of pivot then neutralize all controls and fly the vertical down line.

OK..........less than 45 degrees to the down line ....quick rudder reversal........neutralize all controls...... hold the down line............. pull out to level flight.

Good!............... I think I've got it..........maybe I'll also try one to the right" (Figure 1-15)

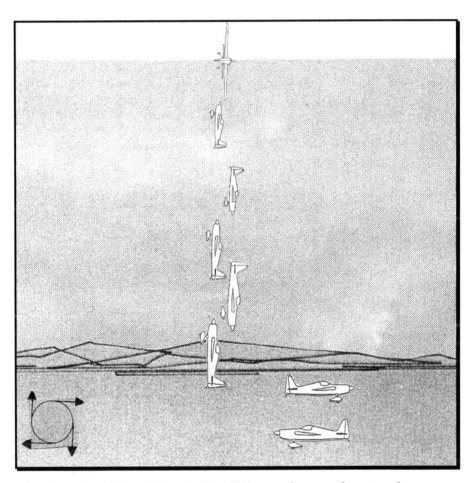

1-15 Hammerhead to the right. How is this different than performing the maneuver to the left?

Hint: Setting the vertical line is the same. Engine and propeller forces are the same however, because you are depressing more and more right rudder on the vertical climb to counter the tightening slip stream you may run out of rudder authority at the pivot. Pivoting earlier and at a higher speed will likely be necessary. The gyroscopic effect of pushing full right rudder causes the nose to go down (move in the direction of the wheels). Adjust the stick position as required to keep the wing tracking along the ground reference. Torque is still trying to roll the airplane to the left so right aileron may be required however, uneven lift at the pivot is trying to tuck the aircraft under and counteracts a portion of the torque effect. Adjusting the position of the ailerons to balance these effects will be necessary.

Most pilots with right turning engines (clockwise as viewed from the cockpit) find pivoting to the left much easier.

Wrap Up

Some days you're hot. Some days you're not. I don't remember when it was I thought I could do a half-way decent hammerhead but it certainly wasn't right away, maybe a hundred or so attempts later. I have since flown many more and in different aircraft. Most now are passable. A few are good, and now and then one feels just right. I'm still looking for the perfect one.

Linda bought me a small toy airplane to carry in my shirt pocket...........she would just as soon I left it there during lunch. It does, however, help me to explain all of this flying stuff. I've dropped it a few times though trying to explain the next maneuver...Spins.

Straight up…Turn around…Straight down. What could be easier?

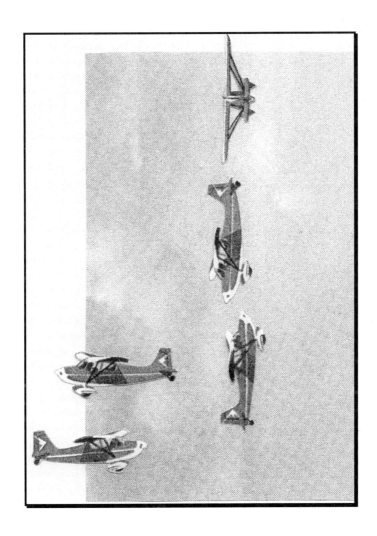

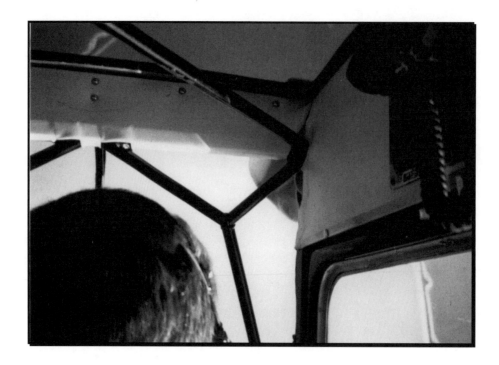

Loss of ground references in the Super Decathlon. There are intersecting roads down there…somewhere.

Chapter 2

The Spin

THE SPIN

It must be that airplanes, especially aerobatic airplanes, when left to their own devices love to spin. Fly them too slow and they stall and spin. Run them out of energy in a maneuver and they want to spin. Mishandle the controls in a botched maneuver and they want to spin. If I didn't know better I would think they would misbehave on the ground as well. I always keep mine securely tied down just in case.

2

THE SPIN

First Experiences

"What are you doing, Dad?" Lara asked in the playful questioning tone of a teenager.

"It's called 'the dance' but some call it 'hand flying'," I explained as I moved in odd turning gyrations on our back yard lawn with my arms held out and elbows bent as if performing a pantomime. I guess I must have looked pretty silly doing flat footed pirouettes, trying to turn 360 degrees repeatedly and still keep my balance. " I'm going flying today to learn s...p...i...n....s." I continued as I whizzed by complete with Doppler effect. Pausing momentarily to let the world catch up with me and stop its whirling, I explained. "Today we are going to learn spins…just wanted to see how hard it is to stay oriented."

"Sure, Dad, I remember how well you do when your riding in something that spins around."

"Don't remind me…but that was just one time," I responded, figuring perhaps stopping now would be a good idea.

The world slowly came back on its axis allowing me to walk a fairly-straight line. Truth was I didn't really know for sure how spinning around and around in an aircraft would effect me. I wasn't particularly worried as there hadn't been any problem with airsickness to date...but this spin stuff...guess I'll find out soon enough, I thought to myself.

"Spins, is it?" I heard a familiar voice from behind me. Turning, I saw my wife Linda motioning with her finger. "Like this?" She questioned.

"Sort of...not that many times I hope." I answered.

"Looks like Dad won't be having lunch with us." Lara stated.

Linda nodded with a smile and then added. "Do we have any film in the camera? I'd like to get a picture of your father's green face."

"Wait 'till he comes back from flying, Mom, then it will really be green." Lara suggested.

Confidence from the female side of the family lacking, and my own less than secure, I headed for the airport with airsickness bag handy, you know, just in case. Thinking back, I recalled spin training as part of the instructions to receive my pilot license. That training consisted essentially of recognizing the stall, initiating a spin and recovering immediately. The spin would not be allowed to develop into several turns. Now, however, we were going to do it with gusto and intent. I was ready...I hoped.

The cool crispness of the early fall morning air was giving way to the warming rays of the sun. The sky was mostly clear of clouds. It was going to be another great day along the Wasatch Front. Foliage around the base of the mountains showed their seasonal display of spectacular colors in hues of orange, yellows, browns and reds mixed with fading greens.

Lewis and I departed Bountiful Skypark in the Super Decathlon and then circled and climbed up over the city. We wanted to climb high enough to cross the Wasatch Front Mountains and into Morgan Valley to the east. As we circled I could make out the black shingled roof of my home nestled in a quit cul-de-sac next to an elementary school. The Great Salt Lake lay to the west, glistening in the morning sun. Interstate Highway 15 stretched north and south between the foothills and the lake with its usual heavy flow of morning traffic. To the north I could make out Lagoon Amusement Park with its Ferris-Wheel, Roller Coaster, and the Midway Strip and The Fun House and other attractions I so enjoyed in my teens. I thought of the modern coaster rides, added in recent years, that would give some sensation of loops and rolls as one raced around the track in predictable fashion. The rails would guide the cars of the coaster and one could generally see what was coming, knowing and feeling full well the car in which you were riding was the moving object and the earth was stationary. I thought of how all that is so different when in an aerobatic airplane. No bolted down gleaming rails to ride on, showing the coming turns. No clickity-clack of the wheels to assure you are on solid structure. No, none of that in an aerobatic airplane tethered to the earth only by gravity and free to move in any direction. No, there is just the sound of the engine and the tug of G-forces when the direction changes…and something else.

We continued to circle over the city climbing to about 8,000 ft msl, just high enough to cross between two mountain peaks and into Morgan Valley. My thoughts returned to flying and the Decathlon. Wow…I reflected, this is so much better than amusement park rides, flying an aerobatic aircraft, pulling G's, tracing figures in the sky, nothing can beat this! I scarcely recalled that one time on the Tilt-a-Whirl where after a hot dog and a coke the struggle between mind and stomach ended in an embarrassing messy affair.

"OK, Ed we're high enough over the valley. Belts tight?" Lewis's voice was loud and clear in the head set and a bit more playful than usual.

"Belts tight," I answered.

"OK follow through with me on the controls, we'll do the first spin to the left. By the way, how long has it been since you have done a spin?" He asked.

Filled with anticipation of what was to come I simply answered it had been a long time. I held the controls lightly and felt the throttle smoothly come back to idle. As the din of the engine noise became more quiet, and quieter still, I could begin to hear the air flowing over the canopy. It was rather like the quite of coasting down a hill in an old car after a noisy climb to the top with a bad muffler.

The nose of the aircraft began to rise steadily, about 30 degrees it seemed, as the control stick moved back towards my lap. The horizon fell away below the nose and all I could see before me was blue sky and a few thin sheets of white clouds with wispy curls. The ride was gentle, quiet, and pleasant. The altimeter read 8,000 feet msl exactly. The compass read due north. All this was about to change...dramatically!

Momentarily the buffeting of an impending stall wobbled the wings. I felt Lewis correcting the movement with some nudges on the rudder pedals. It was as if the little airplane was asking, "do you want to fly or not?"

"Not!" Was the answer with full back stick and full left rudder.

For just a split second, there seemed to be no response of the plane at all and then, like a sudden unexpected strong gust of wind that tosses and whirls things about, the action began.

The nose dropped like a dead weight through the horizon and I could now see the base of the mountains and portions of the valley. The aircraft seemed to bank to the left at the same time, but I wasn't really sure. I felt the stick full back in my lap against the harness buckles and the left rudder pedal fully depressed.

"Heeee..haaa"......came the jubilant voice from the back seat. I wanted to respond with in kind excitement but could only muster a groan. I looked straight ahead and saw the valley below rushing by the cockpit in a blur. I knew we must be rotating yet the sensation was more that the airplane was stationary and the valley floor was somehow spinning like a painter's palette with splashes of color all blended together. My eyes strained to catch up with the movement, which seemed to be to the right. That must be the direction we are rotating I reasoned. It was like looking at the ground out the side window of a moving car. All I have to do, I thought, was fix my gaze further away and the blur would stop. It didn't! We can't be turning right anyway, how could that be, this is a spin to the *left* isn't it?

Lewis counted out the rotation. "Half............one................one and a half............two..........recover." This struggle between mind and stomach ended none too soon as I felt Lewis push full right rudder, bring the stick forward, then neutralize rudders. We were how in a dive and heading straight down. The earth had stopped its movement and the blur of greens and browns, yellows and reds, were replaced with approaching images of trees and hills, hayfields and foliage. I glanced at the airspeed indicator expecting it to be approaching red line...it wasn't. We pulled out of the dive and the throttle was returned to full power. We were again flying straight and level. The altimeter read something below 7,000 ft.

"How are you feeling?" The voice from the back seat asked.

"OK," was my less than sure response.

"Good, let's gain some altitude and try another one." With that, Lewis pulled back smoothly on the stick and the familiar G's of a loop pressed me firmly against my seat cushion. We rolled upright and leveled off at the top of the half loop, gaining about 500 ft. and loosing most of our speed. "OK, your airplane, just circle back up to 8,000 ft." Lewis instructed.

As we slowly climbed up again over the valley I was still trying to figure out why the direction of the spin seemed so confusing to me. Posing my question of spin direction to Lewis he just chuckled a bit, knowing that mind over stomach was really my problem at the moment, and then answered. "Let's just fly around a bit and take some deep breaths."

Enjoying the gentle climbing turns and thinking this aerobatic stuff might be for someone else the unpleasantness in my stomach began letting up. I really didn't want to see my breakfast again and for a moment had some real concerns. Feeling a bit better I leveled off at 8,000 ft.

"We'll try one to the right, but this time look at the controls and just glance outside and straight ahead," came the instructions over the intercom. I pointed the nose north, and began slowing the Decathlon by reducing power as we had done before. The stick moved steadily back, holding altitude at 8,000ft. Buffeting at stall was distinct but short-lived as right rudder was pushed full in and the stick was pulled full back into my lap and held there (Figure 2-1 and 2-2).

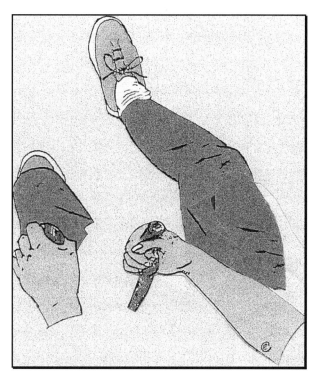

2-1 Full back stick. Full right rudder.

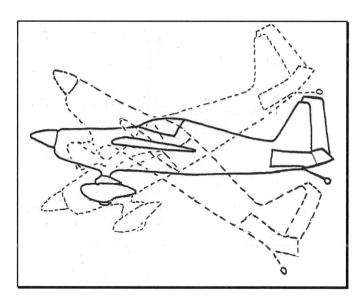

2-2 At the moment of an impending upright slow speed stall the nose rises as the stick is brought full back then falls as lift from the wings is lost.

Following my given instructions, I looked at the controls. I could sense the dropping nose of the aircraft and part roll to the right followed by the yaw. No doubt about it, the plane had to be spinning to the right.

"Half.....one....." Came the count loud and clear in my headset. I looked up............the earth was rotating...*left*. "One and a half."...........I looked back in the cockpit, we were definitely turning... *right*. "Recover!" I looked up and straight ahead as full opposite rudder was applied. We began to slow and then the rotation stopped as the stick was brought forward to the neutral position and the rudders also neutralized. At that moment, while holding and manipulating the controls, the sensation that it was the plane spinning, and not of course the earth racing around below was realized. This matched what I felt and what I saw. Pulling out of the dive I heard. "How are you feeling?"

"I think maybe I've had enough for today."

"OK let's head back."

Kinder words were never spoken. On the ride back, Lewis talked about angles of attack and stalls and autorotation and spin axis and stuff like that. I was still thinking about the sensation of rotating opposite to the spin direction.

With the Decathlon safely stowed away in the hangar I headed for home. Smiling broadly I entered the house, unused airsickness bag in hand. "What's for lunch?" I asked.

REFLECTIONS

The challenge of mind over stomach had been won...at least this time. I hadn't become airsick, well not really sick, and I had learned some of the mechanics of spinning an airplane. Perhaps this aerobatic stuff is not so tough after all, I thought.

Encouraged to learn as much as I could about spins, I hit the books and talked to Lewis and to other pilots. I wanted to figure out how to stay oriented, and safe, while spinning an aerobatic aircraft. There was a lot to learn. Let's take a look at what was discovered.

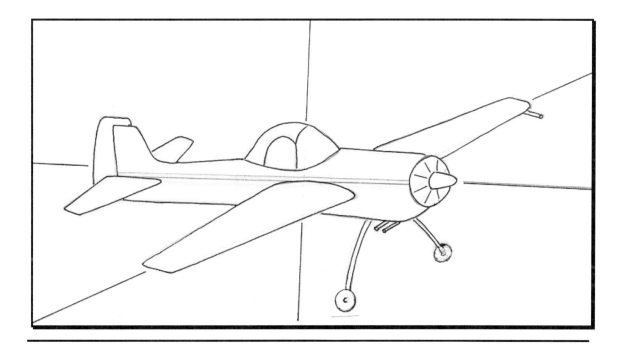

2-3 Yak 55M. An aircraft has three main axis. These include the vertical axis, which passes through the center of the aircraft from top to bottom. Movement around this axis causes yaw. The horizontal axis passes through the aircraft form wing tip to wing tip. Movement around this axis causes pitch. The longitudinal axis passes through the aircraft from nose to tail. Movement around this axis causes roll.

Understanding spins

To better understand this important aerobatic figure let's look at the dynamics of a spin from several different view points. First consider that an aircraft has three main axis including the vertical (yaw axis), the horizontal (pitch axis), and the longitudinal (roll axis). See (Figure 2-3). Spins are an autorotation around an aircrafts axis, usually the vertical axis but it can also be around the horizontal axis. This autorotation evolves into dynamic forces that become, what has been referred to as, the spin axis. The aircraft continues to turn (rotate) around this axis until correct control inputs arrest the autorotation. An aircraft in this situation has experienced changes in pitch, roll and especially yaw. Because of the unequal angle of attack on each wing in a spin, one wing is stalled and one wing is mostly stalled but developing some lift. The relative wind (the air flowing over the aircraft) is now mostly from below, there is little forward momentum as the aircraft falls and rotates earthward. To picture this look at (Figure 2-4), and (Figure 2-5).

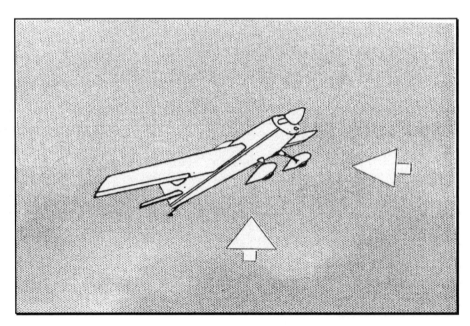

2-4 The aircraft is stalled, banked, and is about to spin. In this configuration the in-spin wing will produce very little lift if any while the out-spin wing will produce some.

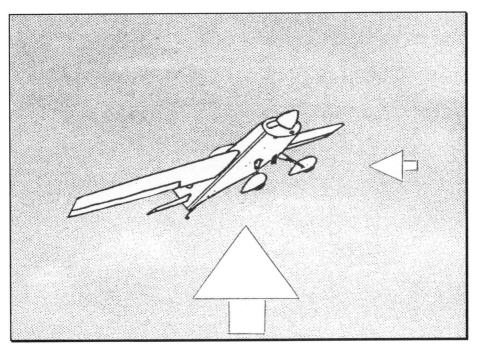

2-5 For a slowed and stalled aircraft about to spin the relative wind from the forward direction is diminishing while the relative wind from below will be increasing.

In an upright spin to the left, the aircraft is first slowed by reducing power and then stalled. The stall is created by increasing the angle of attack (AOA) of both wings by pulling back on the stick and destroying lift. The nose is then skid to the left by depressing full left rudder (the tail skids to the right). This action causes the left wing (the inside wing) to move more slowly as compared to the right wing (outside wing) as the plane now begins to rotate (spin). The faster moving outside (right) wing develops some lift as it races around the arc of the spin. The aircraft essentially stabilizes in this configuration. The wind over the tail (the tail is moving to the right) tends to hold the rudder in its fully depressed position to the left with a sort of suction effect, which increases as the rate of rotation increases. The uneven angle of attack tends to hold the inside wing stalled (in-spin wing) while partial lift from the outside wing (out-spin wing) continues to keep it racing in a circle.

The unequal AOA on the wings holds the aircraft banked left and yawing around its vertical axis. This stalled, banked, yawing configuration becomes the spin axis and the aircraft will remain here at essentially a stable rate of rotation unless something is done to change the axis and/or arrest the rotation.

In this example, we are upright and spinning counterclockwise, having initiated this direction by fully depressing the left rudder (Figure 2-6). The relative wind is mostly from below and we are dropping at the rate of 300 ft to 500 ft per 360 degrees of rotation. Looking over the nose, or slightly to the left, the ground below tends to flash by the canopy appearing to move from our left to our right. If we are able to pick out a prominent object on the ground we see it come into view first to our left, and then pass out of view to our right.

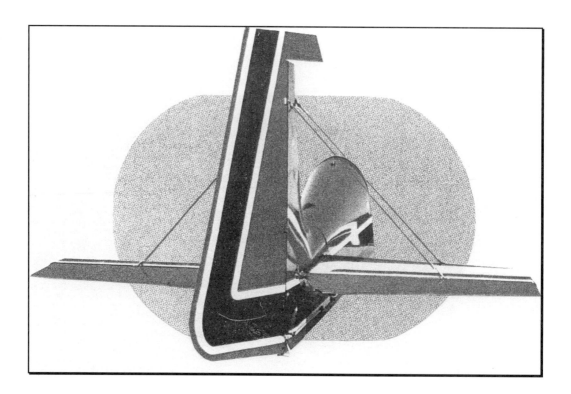

2-6 Extra 230. Full left rudder.

Think of the direction the earth appears to be moving as a giant arrow. In this case, it is pointing to the right. This is important as we shall see in a moment. (Figure 2-7).

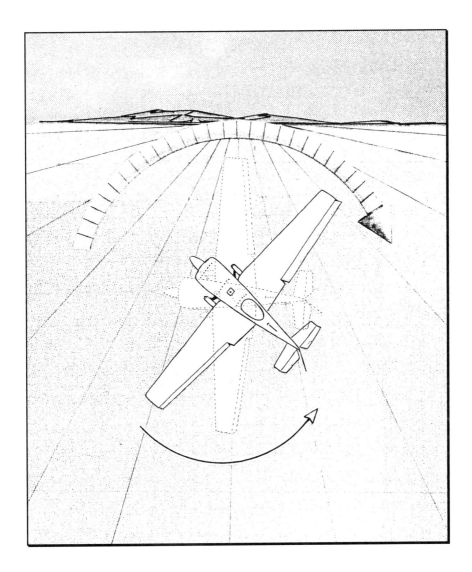

2-7 When in a spin, think of the direction distant objects on the ground move across the canopy as a giant arrow pointing to the rudder to push to freeze the picture and stop the spin.

We are in a left footed, upright spin, rotating counterclockwise, which is the direction in this case, appreciated by the pilot and by an observer on the ground. The direction of the spin is emphasized here because we must know absolutely the direction we are spinning if we are to recover in a timely fashion.

In our example, we know we initiated the spin with left rudder so to stop the rotation we need to depress full opposite (right) rudder. Situations can arise however in which a spin develops with no deliberate initiation with rudder. When this happens, knowing which rudder is the opposite rudder and needing to be pushed becomes a challenge. A choice needs to be made which will be either 100% correct or 100% incorrect. If altitude is becoming a rapidly depleting commodity, then making the correct choice the first time is imperative. If not frozen by fear, the pilot can pick up clues as to which direction the aircraft is rotating by looking at the ground and observing distant prominent objects, such as hills or lakes, as they flash across the canopy. Remember the giant arrow. It always points to the rudder needing to be depressed to stop the spin. Always............ upright or inverted! (Figure 2-8).

Super Decathlon cockpit. Which rudder? One of them needs to be pushed to the floor and held there to stop the spin!

2-8 The Rule of the Arrow applies whether upright or inverted. In this example, both aircraft are spinning counterclockwise. The pilot in the upright aircraft is holding Left rudder. The pilot in the inverted aircraft is holding Right rudder.

The Rule of the Arrow

To test this Rule of the Arrow lets set up an upright spin to the left. Suppose we are headed due north at 0 degrees and straight ahead is a mountain range. To our right at 90 degrees is a large farm. Behind at 180 degrees is a lake. To our left at 270 degrees is open land. (Figure 2-9, page 55). Remember we will be rotating to the left, so the first prominent land mark we see will be the open land as we rotate while looking straight ahead. Next, coming into view to our left, will be the lake and it will pass out of view across the canopy to the right. To stop the spin we want to freeze the reference point in our field of view. To do this we push right rudder at the appropriate time and stop the action.

Suppose in our example of a spin to the left we wanted to make two turns and stop exactly on a northerly heading. We would begin by heading due north towards the mountain , as we rotated in the spin we would see below us first the open land followed by the lake, then the farm, and finally the mountain again as we made one complete revolution. Repeating this sequence we would then make ready to recover as the farm came into view for the second time. Some aerobatic aircraft need a bit of lead time to stop exactly on point so the recovery process needs to begin about a quarter of a turn early, sometimes more, depending on the speed of rotation and number of turns.

Spin recovery

Spin recovery is a much-debated topic among aerobatic pilots. There are many techniques. Most would agree however that a method for emergency spin recovery set forth by Gene Beggs and the late Eric Müller is worth memorizing. This four-step method includes: 1) reduce power to idle. 2) let go of the stick completely. 3) depress the opposite rudder fully. 4) recover from the dive. Let's look at these suggestions more closely.

In a stabilized spin the two things that are going to exacerbate the rotation are power and a change in the spin axis. The two controls that effects these are the throttle and the stick. Increasing the throttle will impart more energy to the spin and make it much more difficult to stop, thus the suggestion to reduce power to idle. The stick controls pitch and bank and it is here that many pilots have difficulty and misuse this control. It seems so logical to level the wings, lift the nose and just fly out of the spin. Attempting this, however, will make things worse, a lot worse! In our example, the aircraft is upright and spinning *left*. It has also rolled into a left bank with the nose below the horizon and it turns in this configuration about its vertical axis. If we try to level the wings by moving the stick to the *right,* we simply flatten the spin and increase the rate of rotation. (Figure 2-10).

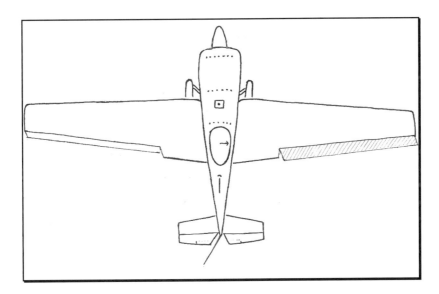

2-10 When in an upright spin to the left...moving the stick to the right flattens the spin and increases the rate of rotation. Conversely, in an upright spin to the right...moving the stick to the left flattens the spin and increases the rate of rotation.

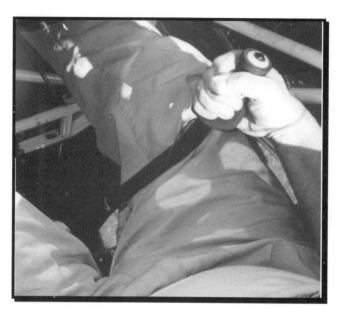

Extra 230   Full Right Stick.

Extra 230 Full Left Rudder, Back Stick.

2-9 In an upright spin to the left with the mountain ahead as the initial reference, the pilot will first see the open land come into view, then the lake, then the farm, and again the mountain as a full turn is completed.

With less bank there is in this situation less drag, sort of an aileron reversal effect and the rotation speeds up. This is not what we want if we are trying to stop the spin. Holding the stick back is certainly not going to lift the nose in a spin. Remember the tail is also rotating and the relative wind is mostly from below. Holding the stick back holds the aircraft in the spin. Movement of the stick in any direction during a well-developed spin is likely to cause more problems than to be of help for the frantic pilot. Thus the suggestion to let go of the stick completely, at least until the rotation has been stopped. With the throttle reduced and the stick released, the pilot can focus on what got him into the spin in the first place...........the rudder.

Depressing and holding the rudder of our stalled aircraft initiated and now maintains the spin rotation. With the spin developed, the suction action of the wind over the deflected rudder tends to hold it in its position. Taking one's foot off the rudder in this situation is not likely to make much of a difference, and will not stop the spin. The action necessary is to fully deflect the rudder in the direction the tail is moving. In this example, the tail is moving to the pilots *right,* so the proper action is to deflect fully the right rudder. This action places the rudder into a portion of the relative wind around the spinning aircraft and acts as a sort of air brake. Only a portion of the rudder is effective. Much of its surface is blocked from the relative wind by the elevator and horizontal stabilizer (Figure 2-11). Looking at the small size of the rudder on many aircraft and considering only a portion is effective in stopping a spin it becomes clear why it takes time to arrest energized rotations. One should not panic if the aircraft continues to turn through an additional one or two rotations in an upright flat spin even with the stopping rudder fully depressed. The pilot needs to get used to the effects of rudder block and the extra rotations and practice these in ideal conditions.

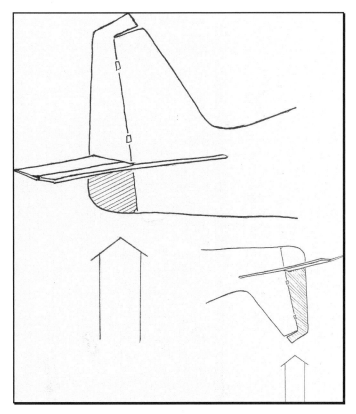

2-11 Only a portion of the rudder is effective in stopping a spin because much of the surface is blocked from the relative wind by the horizontal stabilizer and the elevator.

With the rotations stopped by our correct actions we still have to unstall the wings and get the aircraft flying. It is now we take hold of the stick and move it decidedly forward to place the aircraft in a dive. This is the quickest way to get air flowing across the wings and at a speed which will maintain flight, be it as it may, flying straight down for the moment........but flying! All that remains now is to pull out of the dive and apply power. For some pilots there may be the temptation to try and bring the nose up by pulling back on the stick after the spin rotations have stopped. This will simply keep the aircraft stalled and if the pilot has not neutralized the rudder at this point, a spin in the opposite direction may result. Adding power before the rotations have stopped and the wings are unstalled will add unwanted energy to a deteriorating situation, making recovery difficult if not impossible.

Memorizing and utilizing this simple and generally effective emergency spin recovery technique is certainly worthwhile. Understanding why it works and executing the steps exactly and in order may save the pilots life.

Unexpected spin entry

Lets go through a spin recovery from an inadvertent entry. Somehow we got too slow on a vertical line and the aircraft has buffeted, wobbled and broken into a rather vicious rotation. Our first sensation is surprise. Fear is pushed back for the moment by the urgency of the situation. We know we have to do something...and do it now! The view from the cockpit straight ahead is at first a blur of colors. There is little sensation of descending, though we realize we are...and rapidly. Instinctively we reduce the power full back, thinking we can restore power when we get this mess sorted out. Realizing our firm grip on the stick has produced unconscious movements in an effort to regain control, but to no avail, we recall the adage to release the stick completely. As unnatural an act as we have ever done...........we let go! The stick remains back and nudges a bit to one side. We are upright. We know a rudder needs to be pushed, but which one? We believe we did not initiate this situation with rudder so there is no obvious opposite one to push. We will either be 100% correct or 100% dead wrong.

Now fear comes rushing to the surface. We feel the flush in our face and the tingle in our hands. Our vision sharpens and for that split second we discern prominent objects on the ground at a distance move across the canopy towards our left as we rotate. Other distant objects on the ground follow, moving out of view to our *left*. We press hard left rudder, it seems to have more resistance then usual. The stick moves forward just past center and stops. Not sure if we have done the correct thing we make ready to try something else, anything else, then, as if a brake had been applied, the aircraft rapidly slows and abruptly stops rotating. We release the rudder pressure. The nose is below the horizon and objects on the ground look uncomfortably large. We don't want them to look any larger and our concern prompts us to want to bring the nose up by grabbing and pulling back on the stick. Fortunately we resist this temptation but rather take a hint as to which way we now need to move the stick by recalling when we depressed the rudder to recover the stick moved forward almost as if it knew where to go. Taking hold of the stick now we move it sharply forward to break the stall, noticing there is almost no resistance to our movement. With building airspeed we now feel the increasing resistance in the stick as we bring it smoothly back and add power to establish straight and level flight. Shaken by the experience we decide to call-it-a-day and land our temperamental little aircraft. Recalling the adage, 'when in doubt sort it out', and perhaps we would add, 'anywhere but in the air,' we figure some hangar flying with friends would be a good alternative, at least for now.

Somehow we got ourselves in an upright clockwise spin (a spin to the right). We are not sure just how but we reason trying to correct the attitude of the airplane against the horizon with rudder....way to much rudder, was likely the cause. While the experience is still fresh in our mind we go through spin dynamics again.

Review

For an airplane to spin it must first be stalled. No stall.....No spin! To stall the aircraft the angle of attack must be increased enough to disrupt the smooth laminar flow of air over the wings, thus destroying lift. Speed is not the significant factor as under certain conditions airplanes can *fly* at very low speeds and *stall* at relatively high speeds. For example, the snap roll, to be discussed in a latter chapter, is really a high speed stall with very fast autorotation.

The Stall

Let's look at the following exercise and think through each step. To begin we climb high, 6,000 feet or more above ground level. The throttle is pulled full back and the engine slows to idle. We are in straight and level flight and begin bringing the stick back. At the moment of stall we know the relative wind meets both wings at the same angle of attack, or almost so, and we have equal lift though the aircraft may want to fall of to the left or right or even straight ahead. The momentum for now continues to be forward. We are at stall or very close to it but we are not in a spin. The stick is not full back and if we can keep the nose pointed straight ahead with minor adjustments of the rudder the aircraft will simply sink, perhaps with a gentle side to side sway. As the stick is brought further back the nose may gently bob up and down as the wings intermittently loose and gain lift.

Pulling the stick full back at this slow speed destroys lift and the sink rate increases. On a perfectly calm day, the wings may remain level but it would not take much to disturb this seemingly stable configuration. Should a wing drop it would be much more difficult to bring it back to level but it can be done with quick control adjustments. If this game of balance is lost, the aircraft may descend in a spiral as it tries to regain flying speed. By keeping the stick in the full aft position the aircraft remains stalled though accelerating and rotating as it spirals earthward. This is not a true spin. The descent is rapid and the number of turns per feet descended is few. Leveling the wings with aileron will do little to rescue us from this precarious deteriorating essentially stalled spiraling descent. We need to get lift back in the wings so we can control the aircraft. We need to release the death grip on the stick and get it forward to break the stall   Remember this lesson of the stick as we will come back to it in a moment.

Getting in............and getting out

Let's set up a stall followed by a spin from straight and level upright flight. We climb high, 8,000 ft. above ground level. The relative wind meets both wings at essentially the same angle and allows for equal lift. The momentum is forward for now but it will soon be split between a forward and a downward vector. Harness belts are tight. The throttle is reduced full back. The aircraft has slowed, and the stick is being brought full back. The nose rises until the angle of attack exceeds the wings ability to produce adequate lift and the nose then drops cleanly through the horizon. At this precise moment we wish to change the angle of attack on one wing. This is accomplished by fully depressing a rudder causing the nose to skid to that side (the tail swings to the opposite side). In this example we depress full right rudder and the right wing drops (we have rolled to the right) the nose skids to the right and autorotation begins. The in-spin right wing moves slower at the inside of the circle and remains stalled compared to the out-spin left wing which races around the outside of the circle developing some lift. Forward momentum declines as downward momentum builds. We are in a spin and rotating around the vertical (yaw) axis and banked to the right. The relative wind from ahead and below catches the fully deflected right rudder and causes the fuselage to swing clockwise. The unequal angle of attack on the wings holds the aircraft banked and rotating. This becomes the stable spin axis configuration.   It is an upright spin to the right initiated by right rudder and rotating clockwise.

Having gotten ourselves into a spin, we now need to be able to get ourselves out.   But how? We need to move the controls and restore power to the engine but what do we do first?

Thoughts rush by at lightening speed. Ok, let's see here, how about we just level these wings with a little left aileron...Oops not that...we're rotating faster. Better try something else...uh...maybe increase the power and just fly out of this. No-No, bad idea...Ok-Ok....got it...full hard forward stick to break the stall. Yikes...what was that? Seemed like we stopped rotating and then started again...faster! This is getting a little scary... everything we do with the stick seems to be the wrong thing ...let's just let go of it for now. Hmm...it's forward. Gosh.......ground features are looking bigger and distant ones are passing across the windscreen from our right to our left...seems like a different view than when the spin started......Time to do something to dance out of this.....but what?......Of course....dance...we've got to use our feet.......Now!

We are still holding right rudder. Though confused about the spin direction we know we must push full opposite (left) rudder. The stick moves aft and is centered...we're slowing....slowing........good... spin stopped.....neutralize rudders least we spin again.

Hey....we're upside down...How did that happen?

Now... we use the stick and move it...aft...to establish a dive and flying speed and aft again to pull out of the dive as we increase power and return to level upright flight.

Love that altitude thing...we still have some below us.

So what happened? The upright spin had been well established when we tried leveling the wings with left aileron. Since we were rotating, the out-spin left wing was moving forward and the in-spin right wing was moving backwards relative to the spin axis as the aircraft descended. Deflecting the left aileron rolled the aircraft into a more flat configuration changing drag and allowing it to slice through the air with greater speed. Had we also increased the power at this point the nose would have come up, thus flattening the configuration even more and dramatically increasing the rate of rotation. Moving the stick slowly forward would have increased the rate of rotation but moving the stick abruptly full forward flipped the aircraft over onto its back. If this had been a single movement it would likely have been easily perceived. The combination of yaw and pitch seems to be less easily appreciated. There was a momentary hesitation as the spin reversed direction. (Figure 2-12). The left wing remained the forward moving out-spin wing but because we were inverted and still holding right rudder the spin direction became counterclockwise. Since it was the depression of a rudder that initiated the spin it was depression of the opposite rudder that stopped it. The stick moved aft and centered. All that remained was for us was to establish flying speed and recover from the dive.

When in a spin, remember to use your feet!

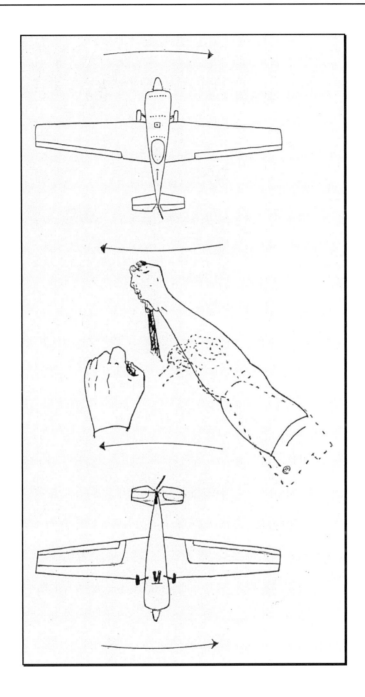

2-12 With the stick full back in an upright spin and holding right rudder the rotation of the aircraft is clockwise. Continuing to hold right rudder and abruptly moving the stick forward flips the aircraft onto its back. The spin direction reverses and now becomes counterclockwise.

Wrap Up

Spins are great fun, we'll talk more about them and some other variations in subsequent chapters and books. In and of themselves spins are not particularly dangerous, unless you are close to the ground, but then any maneuver performed within a stones throw of terra firma is inherently dangerous, even landing. Having an "out" when things go bad, or are not quite right, and knowing what to do and when to do it keeps pilots healthy and their aircraft in one piece. Inverted spins tend to recover more quickly than upright spins in most aircraft. Practice spins high above ground level, remember altitude above you is a useless commodity.

Learning aerobatics can be a challenge. Take time to reread this chapter, it's an important one. Look also at the list of books in the bibliography. They are highly recommended reading.

Next, we'll talk about rolls. Hang on to your seat as this can be quite a ride, especially when things go wrong.

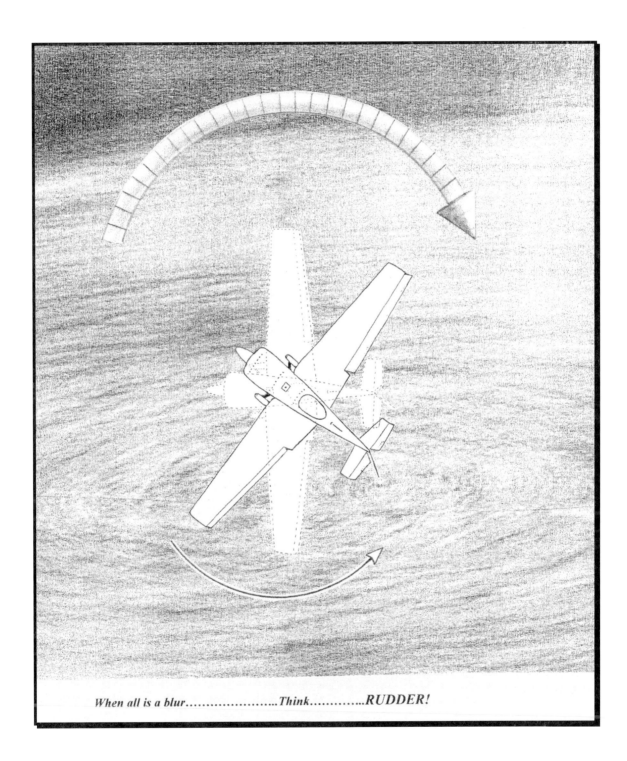

When all is a blur..........................Think...............RUDDER!

Chapter 3

The Roll

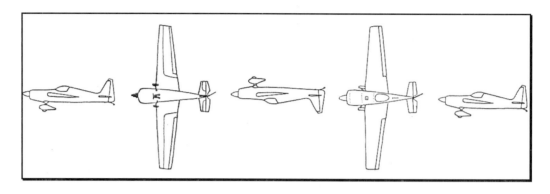

There are very good rolls…the kind you see at air shows and aerobatic competitions

There are bad rolls…and there are very bad rolls…those that start as a roll and end up

entirely something else.

3

THE ROLL

First Experiences

"RIGHT RUDDER, PUSH and LEFT RUDDER, PULL." Lewis's instructions seemed simple enough. All I had to do to perform a horizontal roll was apply left aileron to initiate the roll while also concentrating on keeping the nose of the airplane just above the horizon. I would be able to keep the nose up by depressing top (right) rudder as the right wing rolled up to the vertical. The left wing would be down so this position I called *Left Knife-Edge*. At the same time, I would need to begin pushing the stick forward as we approached the inverted position. This was the "Right Rudder, Push" portion of the maneuver. Simple! Now from the inverted position and still holding left aileron to continue the roll, it would just be a matter of again concentrating on keeping the nose just above the horizon. Depressing top (this time left) rudder as the left wing comes up thru vertical with the right wing down at *Right Knife-Edge* and, at the same time, pulling the stick back to neutral as the airplane completes the roll to level flight. This was the "Left Rudder, Pull" portion of the maneuver. No sweat! (Figure 3-1).

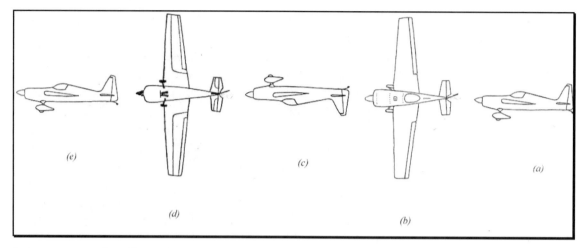

3-1 *Horizontal roll to the left. Begin with straight and level flight. For some lower powered aircraft it may be helpful to pitch the nose up slightly (a) Applying left aileron rolls the left wing down (left knife-edge). Top rudder and some forward stick is necessary to hold the nose of the aircraft on point (b). Continuing the roll to inverted now requires forward stick to keep the nose up (c). At right knife-edge, top rudder is again required (d). The roll is complete with return to straight and level flight (e).*

I followed through on the controls as Lewis demonstrated a couple of rolls to the left calling out positions and movements of the rudder and stick. Easy, I thought. Sort of like loosening a post in the ground by just moving it forwards and backwards as you shift your weight from one foot to another rhythmically. Piece of cake!

We did a couple more rolls linked together....top (right) rudder into the knife edge along with forward stick through inverted, then left (top) rudder along with back stick and return to level flight and then repeat the whole thing again. It was smooth and coordinated throughout with more of a blending of control inputs rather than any abrupt singular movements. We were back on point and flying along the shores of the Great Salt Lake. A ridge on Promitory Point Peninsula lay along the horizon across a portion of the lake and served as a reference.

"Lets climb a bit....your airplane, I'll check with Salt Lake Approach for traffic, I haven't heard any calls have you?"

"No," I answered, and began scanning the sky. The old radar system at Salt Lake Center did not pick us up very well below 8,000 ft above sea level. We were cleared to maneuver along the shores of the Great Salt Lake west of Ogden. The ILS approach path into Salt Lake was a safe distance to the east from our position. VFR traffic was intermittent and we kept an eye out for them and frequently announced our position. Hill Air Force Base was to the southeast of us. F-16 jet fighters, along with just plain big and fast Air Force planes going to and from the base would whiz by, at a distance, but almost always unannounced. They should not be anywhere near us but we wanted to make sure. I made left and right clearing turns and then lined up on our reference point.

"All right, smooth and easy, stay on the point....go ahead."

I pulled the nose up slightly on the Super Decathlon and pushed the stick far over to begin a roll to the left. Looking straight ahead I wondered what happened to the reference point. It was just there a second before.

"Right rudder…more right rudder." Lewis was yelling, I think more than twice. His voice got a bit louder. "Forward stick, get the stick forward..........Whoa......OK my airplane."

Roll going bad from the inverted position in the Super Decathlon.

All I could see looking straight ahead was water. The noise of the air going by the canopy was getting louder, muffling the noise from the engine. We were going really fast! Lewis had the controls and had pulled the throttle all the way back, I was plastered to my seat and could hardly move. I felt the G forces build and my vision become less and less clear, sort of indistinct and fuzzy around the edges.

Colors seemed to fade and everything looked gray. Lewis was saying something about red-line but he might as well have been talking to a wall as I gave no answer. The sensation was strange, I could hear much better than I could see, but then things gradually began sounding more and more distant and faint. For a moment, I felt suspended in space and time. Then suddenly, it seemed, the noise of the engine was loud again. Vision returned quite quickly and I could see sky and earth coming back into view and in their proper positions. For a few seconds, perhaps longer, there was no sense of being at their controls of an airplane, no cognitive processing, just a blank thoughtless motionless nothing. The G forces were gone but the feeling of confusion was not.

"Look at the altimeter." Lewis's voice jarred me from my blank stare.

I looked. We had lost over 800 feet. I searched the horizon for our reference...the ridge on Promitory Point. It was strangely gone. Still somewhat confused I kept searching, then it dawned on me.........we had somehow reversed directions.

"Well that was an accelerated split-S, how did you like it?" He questioned. (Figure 3-2)

"Not much," I answered.

"Me either," let's head for home."

G-Meter Super Decathlon

3-2 *The Split-S is a maneuver that brings the aircraft from inverted to upright by completing a downward arc similar in appearance to half of the letter 'S'. When unplanned or unexpected the speed build-up and loss of altitude to complete the arc can be alarming.*

Back safe on the ground we did a post-flight inspection of the plane checking struts, ribs, fabric, and just about everything that attaches the wings to the fuselage. We had pulled 5.5 G's on the old Decathlon coming out of that dive.

"I've heard of wings being pull completely off and seen some cracked ribs after a split S like that, best we pull some inspection plates and have a real good look." Lewis suggested. We did. Everything looked fine.

From a simple roll to totally stressing the plane, and near black out for me, and it all happened very fast. I knew I had to understand what went wrong.

"You need to be on top of what is happening with the aircraft, so you can feed in the proper amount of control at the proper time. You were just too far behind the action." Lewis suggested.

"About how far?" Seemed a logical question.

"Well, judging from our speed in that dive, I would say at least a mile....maybe more."

He was right. I realized that when I started the roll by applying full left aileron the airplane rapidly began turning on its side. Now instead of the wings being horizontal and developing lift to support flight, they were turned vertical with the right wing pointed skyward and the left wing pointed towards the ground. The side of the fuselage, not a very good wing, could not develop enough lift to support flight. Despite the efforts of the spinning propeller, the aircraft wanted to descend. To counteract this, top rudder, the one pointing skyward, needed to be depressed.

This flight was over...learning more about rolls, however, was just beginning.

Reflections

When I began the roll I made two initial mistakes, and more when things started going bad. The rate at which a roll develops and is maintained depends on how much the ailerons are deflected. I pushed the stick hard to the left. This initiated a fairly fast roll. Too fast for me to keep up with and still hold the nose on point. I needed top (right) rudder immediately. Not enough, quick enough, and we were headed down. As we rolled to inverted, with the nose dropping below the horizon, I now needed lots of forward stick to push the nose up. Far behind the action I had allowed the plane to descend.....and rapidly accelerate. We were now inverted with the nose dropping way below the horizon and the plane picking up a lot of speed under full power. What to do next?

The wings of the Decathlon would not be able to withstand a lot of negative G's. Pushing the stick hard forward from this accelerating inverted position might risk exceeding the negative G limits and cause the wings to fold around the fuselage in a metal embrace. By now we were approaching a near vertical descent. Despite reducing power by pulling the throttle all the way back, the speed of the plane was approaching redline. Our only hope.........bring the stick back smoothly and thus upright the plane by completing a descending arc...... and hope the speed and positive G's would not exceed the strength of the hardware holding the wings to the fuselage, least they depart and we become a sky borne toboggan....heading straight down.

The waters of The Great Salt Lake below seemed to deceive judgment as to our height.

Where we to low to complete the arc?

Fortunately the wisdom of, *altitude below the airplane is like money in the bank*, paid off again....we had enough.

The roll seemed like such an easy thing to do. Not so! Horizontal flight can be lost to a screaming dive in seconds. Having enough altitude allowed us to recover without overstressing the plane. The speed build up, however, was surprising to me...it was very rapid.

For the next several flights we broke this so called simple slow roll down into its basic parts. In the Decathlon the nose is brought up just above the horizon, then the plane is rolled to knife-edge. This is a smooth deliberate movement, but not to fast. Aileron pressure is continued and there is a blending of a touch of forward stick accompanied by firm top rudder to hold the knife-edge position, but only for a second or so. The Decathlon does not fly well on its side and wants to descend despite all efforts to keep it at knife-edge.

Lying on your side, while controlling the flight path of an airplane, feels rather awkward. In this position, it is easy to move the controls in the wrong direction or apply too much input on one and not enough on another. For example, in level upright flight pulling back on the stick will bring the nose up and the airplane will climb, but in *Left Knife-Edge flight* (left wing pointing earthward) pulling back on the stick will move the nose counterclockwise and into a descending spiral. (Figure 3-3)

With a little practice I could see I needed to do whatever was necessary to keep the nose up and on point. If that was to apply top rudder, and it felt like a lot of top rudder, then that's what I did. The voice from the back seat followed my movements. "More right rudder, more...... forward stick...not to much.......now blend in left rudder......keep the nose on point and the roll going.......ease the stick back.....a little more.......better.......try another one."

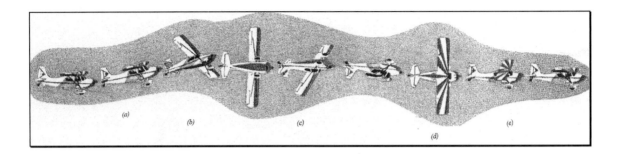

Full roll to the left from level flight. 15 degrees up (a), blend in right rudder (b), blend out right rudder and begin forward stick (c), left rudder (d), back stick (e).

Right rudder …Push...Left rudder…Pull.

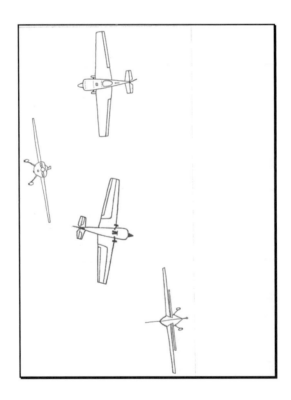

3-3 Pulling back on the stick when at knife-edge will initiate a spiral......and other surprises.

Right Rudder Push...Left Rudder Pull, was not mechanical at all, it was more like a gliding motion. It felt good the times I could get it just right. Slow rolls can be anything but slow. With full aileron deflection they are over before you know it and the amount of rudder and elevator applied may be more pressure than large movements. If the timing is right, several rolls can be linked together. The earth and sky seem to swing around the nose of the plane in a kaleidoscopic dizzy display. After a dozen or so rolls in one direction it is a good idea to add a couple in the opposite direction, at the end, to stop the sensation of continuing to roll (and to keep your stomach in its proper place). The slower the roll the more blending of control movement is required. A super slow roll, one in which the rolling motion is barely perceptible, may seem easy but is actually a very challenging maneuver. Lewis was good at this.

From the inverted position thru right knife edge (right wing pointing earthward) to upright seemed to give me the most problem. It was a matter of keeping in enough left aileron to keep the roll going so I could blend in top (now left) rudder and ease the stick back at the proper rate. For some reason I would ease off left aileron and the roll would slow down or stop. After a bit of practice I could see that the speed of the roll could be varied by the amount of aileron deflected. As this happened the amount of rudder and elevator movements also needed to be varied.

Wrap Up

After a few more flights I was starting to get the hang of it. No more unintentional split-S's! The cramped cockpit was becoming a bit more comfortable and I was beginning to feel less and less intimidated by the unexpected. It was like I had mentally moved myself forward in the cockpit and ahead of the aircraft. My thoughts had previously been far behind the plane, like a towed banner flapping in the breeze. I had been reacting to events rather than being with, or ahead, of the action. Now my movements on the controls were becoming more deliberate and exact. I was making the airplane go where I wanted it to go...and this felt a lot better.

On our flights to and from the practice area Lewis would have me do stick and rudder coordination exercises. The goal was to move the nose of the plane along lines of a geometric figure or letter and thus trace out, for example, a square or triangle in the sky. Using the nose of the airplane as a pencil and the sky as a sheet of paper and trying to write my name felt like kindergarten all over again.

Putting, and keeping, the nose of the airplane exactly where it needs to be is the trick to doing a good roll.

This maneuver is a lot of fun. When the timing is just right it seems you can keep the roll going and going and going.

Loops are discussed in the next chapter. One of the first aerobatic maneuvers to learn it is by no means the simplest to do well. A perfectly round loop is more rare than common. Read on to see why.

Chapter 4

The Loop

THE LOOP

It could be said the shortest distance between two points is a curved line.

It could also be said a circle is made up of straight lines connected at their ends by the same angle.

Both statements are true......and false.

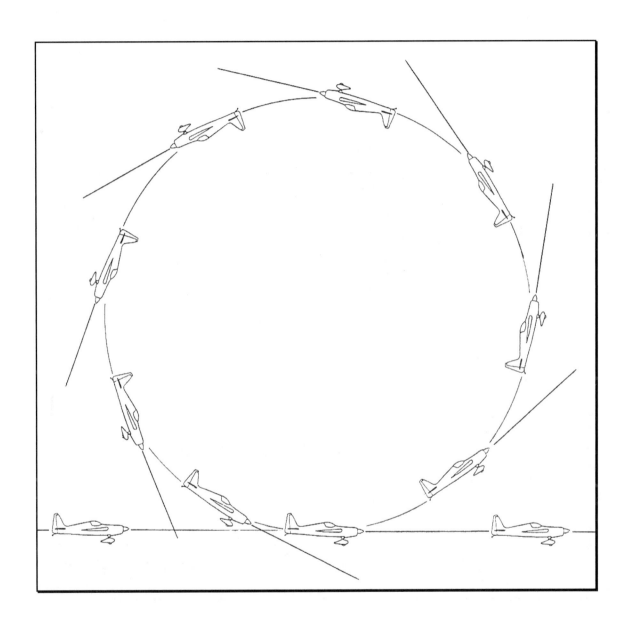

THE PERFECT LOOP

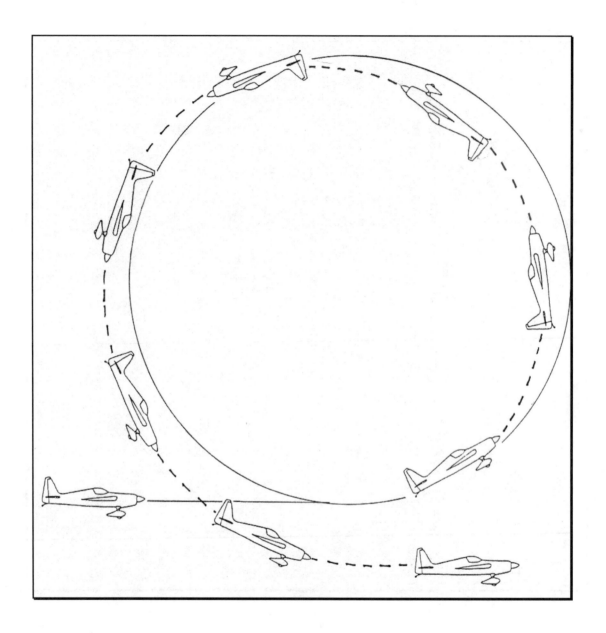

4

LOOPS

Oh! No! I am dead...again!

The altimeter stabilized after a moment or so. Sure enough, the dials indicated fifty or so feet below the above ground level elevation I had planned.   I had set 2000 feet as the hard deck or absolute lowest point. Dang…plowed another long furrow, good thing it was just across the sky and not in some farmers' field, I thought to myself.

Leveling the wings again at exactly 2000 feet above ground level and setting the airspeed at exactly 160 miles per hour I pulled back on the stick and attempted yet another loop, a figure I had practiced many times.

The familiar G forces pressed my backside firmly against the tightly packed parachute that served also as my seat. My goal was to carve a perfect circle in the sky gaining exactly 500 feet at the apogee. The altimeter would then read exactly 2500 feet above ground level.   Returning to my starting altitude it would read exactly 2000 feet. Gravities' heavy hand would snatch away three fourths of my speed by the time I completed the ascending side of the circle. Now inverted, I would float across the top of the loop for just a moment.   Speed and G forces would quickly build on the descending side of the circle being greatest just as I pulled to level flight. I should come out of the loop at my starting speed and altitude. That was the plan.

The slipstream of the propellers blast at my starting point had not completely dissipated within the few seconds it took to fly the loop, so when I returned to level flight I encountered this disturbed air. It caused a distinct 'bump' much the same as encountering uneven pavement on a highway.   That's got to be a better loop, must be back at my starting altitude, I reasoned.

Looking with anticipation at the altimeter I expected the dials to fix on 2000 feet exactly above ground level. They did not.   Tapping the glass over the dials also did not make any difference. I was still not pegging the altitude at the completion of the loop. Why, I wondered.

I tried the loop again. Aligning the nose of the aircraft with the straight road below I leveled the wings and checked them by looking from side to side to see that each wing tip lay equidistant relative to the horizon. The old Decathlon needed a bit more speed so I pushed the nose down slightly until the airspeed was 160mph and again leveled the wings. "OK, Pull, Set, Hold." I said to myself out-loud.

Altimeter (dial on the left) in the Super Decathlon.

The view straight ahead of earth and sky gave way to seemingly nothing but endless clear blue as if everything of contrasting shapes and colors had vanished. The forces of gravity, so distinctly felt at the initial pull on the control stick, were now all but gone. Any sense of being upright or inverted seemed to blur with a feeling of total suspension, as if only my thoughts and awareness had substance and nothing else. Hoping to find a more familiar world I tipped my head as far back as I could to look out of the top of the canopy.

Within a moment I was able to pick up the returning, but disturbingly different, view of sky and earth turned upside down. Building G forces brought back weighty physical awareness as I strained against the effects of my 160 pounds begin to double and would double again by the time I reached the bottom of the loop. Now the peaceful blue of the summer sky was rapidly diminishing. I turned my gaze straight ahead. The inverted horizon flashed by and there was nothing to see but deep hard shades of brown and green.

Shapes of hills and valleys took form as did the road now directly below me. The increasing speed of the aircraft and pressures on the control stick caused muscles to tighten.

What had been near bliss at the top of the loop was now becoming tense anxiousness. I fixated on the road and watched its appearance lengthen until it met the horizon. I began to relax some.

It's just the back side of the loop, nothing to get worked up about. I told myself as the aircraft returned with a bump through the slipstream to straight and level flight. The altimeter read 1900 ft above ground level. I'm getting better at making things worse it seemed.

Rather than the perfect loop, I was repeating the perfect mistake. After a few more tries but with not much improvement I decided to 'call it a day' and head back to the airport.

Safe on the ground I set to thinking about the problem of flying the airplane in a vertical circular path called a loop. The problem must be the radius, I figured. It simply made sense, vary the radius, even slightly, and the shape of the circle changes. I looked up the definition of a circle. Paraphrasing; a circle is a curved geometric plane equidistant from a fixed center and the line segment joining the center of a circle with any point on its circumference is the radius. The flight maneuver in which the aircraft flies a circular (shaped like a circle) path is the loop. If somehow the airplane could be tethered to the center of the circle then the circle would be perfectly round every time. Like a ball swinging at the end of a rope.

Thinking of other objects one might swing in a circle I chuckled to myself as I recalled an incident from my youth. My thoughts began to wander leisurely from the present back to one particular summer day, long past.

I could not have been very old, maybe eight or nine. On occasion my brother, and I would be left with our grandparents on their small farm just at the city limits in the small northern Utah town of Smithfield.

It was one of those easy chore days, you know, not really much work to do and lots of time to do other things. Plenty of opportunity for an older brother to teach his younger, and mostly gullible, sibling a thing or two of how the world is and all the exciting things you can do, if you dare.

We had just finished milking the cows. I helped some by pouring the warm fresh milk into the large stainless steel container from the milking bucket. Soon and the job was done, the container was full, and there was about half-a-bucket of milk left over. So we headed up the trail to the farmhouse, maybe a quarter of a mile away.

Maurice was swinging the bucket 'to-n-fro' as we walked along, taking care not to spill the frothy contents. He, being bigger and older, could swing the bucket impressively with great skill and control. Each swing going just a bit higher and then stopping the undulations at will.

"Want to try?" he asked.

"Sure!" My response was enthusiastic and incautious.

The bucket, more full than empty, seemed a bit heavy to go swinging around like that, but I wasn't about to say so. It seemed easy at first, just back and forth but the weight of the whole thing put me slightly off balance with each higher swing. I managed to get the swinging stopped finally with only some minor spillage and then awkwardly set the bucket and its contents down.

"If you swing the bucket hard enough it will go all the way around and you won't even spill a drop," He explained. "It's this centrifugal force or something. Anyway you need a good wind-up to make it all the way around like this," and he gestured with his arm cocked high behind him. "Just get a few swings to start and then swing it really hard and around you go…you can do it," he encouraged as he stepped back a pace or two supposedly to give me swinging room.

I took a firm grip on the handle and glanced at my brother's assuring nods. I then started to swing the old bucket.

"Harder, harder, now real hard," came his encouraging shout.

With one last mighty pull on the handle, the bucket and its contents headed skyward. The handle tensed hard and my fingers and arm tensed harder. The momentum of the weighted bucket pulled me forward and to the side. The bucket began rising high over my head, almost taking me with it. I hung on but that did not seem to be the right thing to do. I looked up but wished I had not.

The swinging motion had stopped directly above my head. My first impulse was to run...to late. I let go the handle as the bucket, its contents, and I crashed to the ground in a splash of white and foam.

Shaken but uninjured, soaked with milk and bewildered, I picked myself up along with the empty bucket and slowly started again up the trail. My brother's uncontrolled laughter summoned our grandparent's attention.

"What happened to you?" Grandma asked in her usual stern tone.

I stood on the farmhouse porch dripping an expanding pool of white onto the floor. Fear frozen I was unable to answer other than gesture with the bent and broken milk bucket dangling from the mostly detached handle.

"You've got some explaining to do young man," she snapped. I opened my mouth to answer but was motionless and mute. Our younger sister Elaine stood behind grandma's skirt peering around the edges, but not to far around, just barely enough to see and hear my scolding.

"It wasn't his fault, I made him do it." My brother blurted, smiling from ear to ear and not a drop of milk on him.

"Made him do what?"

"Well it was kind of this experiment with gravity," He began.

Just then, Grandpa entered the scene showing his usual unruffled and calm ambience. I suppose that is something that comes with a lifetime of experiences.

"Milk didn't stay in the bottom of the bucket...again, 'specially half way around." He said without emphasis or expression. "Well clean up your mess."

And that was that!

Reflections

With my thoughts back to the problem at hand, it became apparent I needed to understand the dynamics of objects moving in a circle against the forces of gravity and the elements.

I had experienced these forces first hand at an early age with the swinging milk bucket episode...and the resulting messy consequences, but with little real understanding of what happened and why.

I wondered; could any similarities be drawn between the mess I was making trying to fly the perfect loop and the mess I had made with the milk bucket.

The Decathlon was not being swung around at the end of control cords like an old style model airplane. It was not held in the loop by an external attachment. Yet some sort of force was acting on it in those loops...a force I could feel.

It wasn't just the force of gravity. It was the continuously changing force of gravity, it seemed, as the airplane moved around the loop…and there were other things.

What where these things? It appeared there dynamic effects needed to be balanced to create the perfect loop. How?

I went to my library and dusted off an old Physics book. As I read about the forces acting on an object in motion I began to reason that should an object move along a straight line it has the physical properties of acceleration and velocity.

Acceleration and velocity are vector rather than scalar quantities, and thus have directional components.

Reading further, I noted that when an object moves in a circular path the velocity vector is continuously changing direction along the curved path and the acceleration vector is directed toward the center of the path being inscribed.

These vectors are present in the loop. Acceleration thus configured is centripetal acceleration.

If this centripetal force should disappear, the object would now move along a straight path tangent to the circle. Like a ball, whirling at the end of a string which breaks and the ball flies off in a straight line (Figure 4-2).

This was getting interesting.

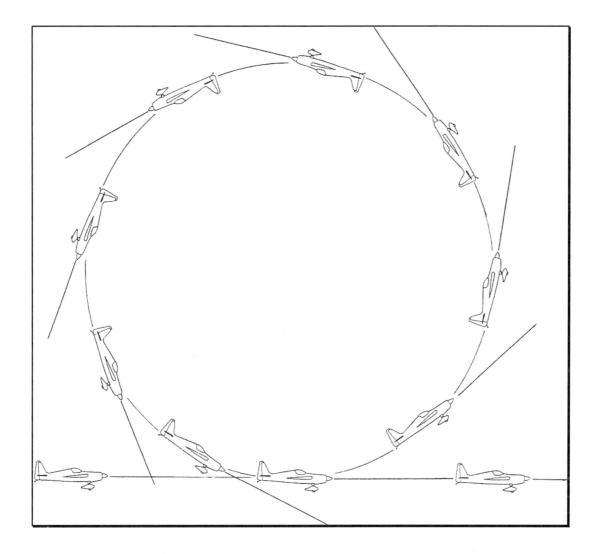

4-2 The aircraft flies along the circular rather than along the tangential lines because the pilot holds back pressure on the stick, which is heaviest on the ascending and descending portions and lightest (even perhaps a bit of forward pressure if needed) over the top. The rate of transition of the aircraft changes between each equidistant point, being rapid on the ascending and descending portions and slowest over the top.

I kept reading and found that when there is non-uniform circular motion of an object, such as an airplane in a loop, the object moves with varying speed in a circular path. Acceleration now has not only a centripetal component but also a tangential component. The force acting on the object also has a tangential and radial component. This tangential component causes the speed of the object to change over time. Thus, the aircraft slows over the top of the loop and speeds up at the bottom of the loop. The tangential component arises from the weight of the object.

When objects rotate in a vertically configured circle it is gravity that provides the tangential acceleration and most if not all of the centripetal acceleration. The resistive force of the air, the medium through which the object travels effects its velocity and if in freefall can eventually limit the speed of the object through the medium.

These resistive forces are countered by the thrust of the aircraft engine. This thrust has varying effects on the tangential component and centripetal component depending on position and direction of the aircraft in the loop.

Now it was all starting to make some sense. I could appreciate these changing forces of speed, direction, and gravity as I flew the aircraft in a loop.

It then became apparent that as an object moves along its vertical circular path the magnitude and direction of the various vectors are continuously changing. In other words, at the top of such a vertically positioned circle the acceleration component is directed toward the center and downward and the weight also directed downward. At the bottom of the circle, weight continues to be directed downward and the acceleration component continues toward the center. OK, that helps explain the reason G forces are least at the top of the loop and most at the bottom (Figure 4-3).

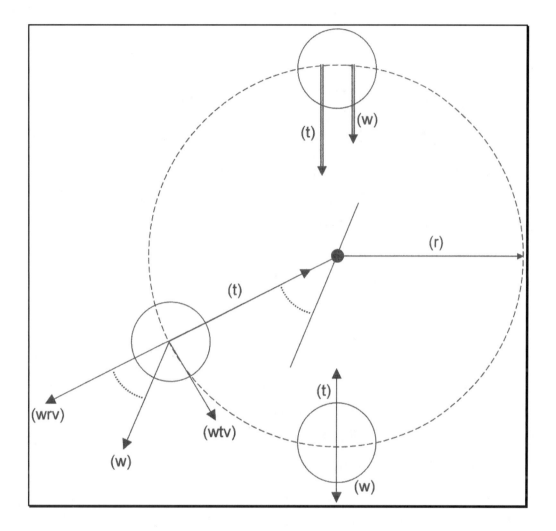

4-3 Suppose we had a heavy ball attached to a cord and swinging in a vertical circle of radius (r). The weight of the ball (w) would always be pointing directly down at the top and bottom of the circle. The speed of the ball is non-uniform around its circular path. As the weighted ball moves around the circle, it has a tangential vector component (wtv) and a radial vector component (wrv). The tension (t) on the cord is greatest at the bottom of the circle and least at the top.

With the seemingly complicated dynamics of the varying forces encountered in the loop reduced to simple Newtonian Law it was now time to see if all this applied to the task of flying the airplane.

The following examples may be helpful. Consider a situation such as swinging a ball attached to a string in a vertical circle. It is easy to see that the string has a force acting on it. You can actually feel the tension in your fingers, which is greatest at the bottom of the arc, so you know it exists. The pull on the string is called centrifugal force. It is balanced by centripetal force. These two forces are equal in magnitude and opposite in direction and satisfy Newton's third law of motion.

In the cockpit, you also feel a force, mostly in the seat of your pants, as you pull into a loop and again as you exit the loop. You now become the ball at the end of the string.

The sensations of increased weight we have come to call G forces. The definition of a G is the force equal to the gravity exerted on a body at rest. Centripetal (inward) forces are necessary to keep you moving along the arc with the airplane. You also feel the effects of these described forces in your hands and fingers as the varying stick pressure necessary to initiate and hold the airplane in the desired arc.

We know from our discussion of non-uniform circular motion we will move with varying speed around the loop. In order to make the loop circular we need to match our control inputs exactly to the dynamics of these continuously changing Newtonian forces.

For purposes of illustration let's set up ideal conditions and go fly a loop. It is a windless summer day. The aircraft is performing flawlessly and we climb to 2500ft above ground level. Diving for needed dynamic energy we level off at 2000ft and 160mph indicated air speed. A firm pull on the stick initiates our desired vertical arc. Like the ball and the string, we have just set the length of the string with that initial pull. We must vary the pressure on the stick but must not vary the length of the string. To do so would make the loop anything but round. Should we relax the stick pressure too much or at the wrong time, we lengthen and flatten that portion of the figure. If we pull or maintain too much pressure, we pinch a portion of the figure. These errors are all very noticeable to any observer on the ground (Figure 4-4).

Extra 230.   Nothing but blue sky ahead.

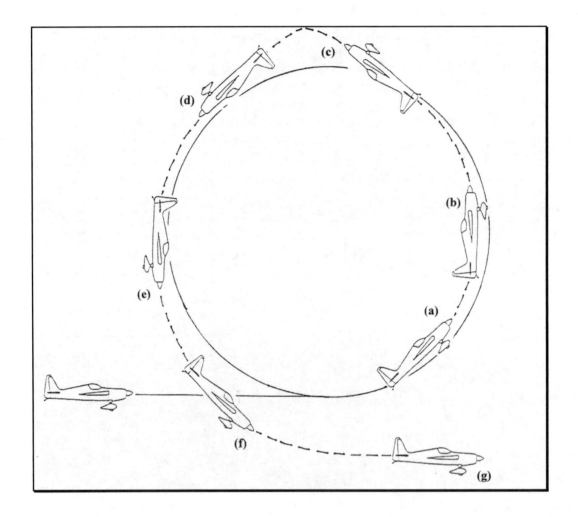

4-4 An egg shaped loop. The pilot pulls a bit too hard initially (a). A perfect, but smaller, circle is still possible if orientation and control inputs are well-managed (b), however the pilot relaxes slightly stick pressures and the loop flattens, the aircraft is running out of energy, the pilot is probably concentrating on finding the horizon (c). Having traversed the apogee the pilot is now concentrating on the reference road below and wondering how much back pressure to apply as the stick position needs to match the initial input (d). Too little too late, speed is building and the back-side of the loop is distorted (e). Buffeting of the residual prop wash is encountered (f), but the exit point is still low (g).

To fly the perfect loop we are faced with many problems, but most, if not all, are solvable. We cannot see the center of the circle but know we must establish and maintain one. We have no string or other means of measuring our distance to the center of the circle to define a radius. No computer draws an arc for us to follow. We are on our own in the cockpit with only our senses to guide us mainly sight, sound, and feel.

Sight

What we see depends on where we look, and where we look is critical and timed in performing a loop. What we see must also have meaning and impact to cause us to take certain actions. Let's examine what we must see, even from our restricted cockpit position, in order to fly a circular loop. Most cockpits of aerobatic aircraft have a compromised view to the outside. One may look directly ahead and to either side but looking directly behind is impossible when firmly strapped in. Forward and, side-to-side, effective range of vision is about 240 degrees even with some neck straining. Vision in the vertical, up-and-down geometric plane is even less, about 120 degrees. The fuselage and wings block a good portion of the pilots view. In straight-and-level flight we are able to see most of the sky, a good portion of the horizon and distant terrain, but not much of the ground below us (clear plastic Lexan floors help some, Figure 4-5). If we attempt to perform a loop by looking only straight ahead we limit considerably the information available to us. We see the ground and horizon fall below the nose of the aircraft as we pull the stick back and begin the loop. Then...nothing...except sky and clouds until we are able to pick up ground references again. This method of ...pull...relax....flop over the top......and pull until level flight inscribes a distorted, egg-shaped, pretzel of a figure that is as close to round as is a football.

4-5 Extra 230. Clear plastic panels on the side and belly of the fuselage aid the pilots view.

Using ground references such as a straight road to line up on when starting and finishing the loop is helpful in keeping the vertical geometric plane so the heading remains the same and we refrain from drawing a curly-Q in the sky. But it does little to assure the shape of the loop is round. We need another visual reference, one that helps us gage position and rate of rotation. That visual reference is the wing tip or sighting device relative to the horizon.

In straight-and-level flight the wing tip lies in a fixed position relative to the horizon. A sighting devise would lie parallel to the horizon. This position is the bottom of the loop. If we watch the wing tip carefully it will inscribe the shape of our loop perfectly. As if we had placed a giant pencil on the wing tip and it drew the shape of our loop on the sky just at the horizon. We could almost envision where the center of the loop would be as we watch the wing tip draw the circumference. The speed or rate at which the circle is drawn varies but the movement of the wing in relation to the horizon and the center of the circle is constant (Figure 4-6)

Let's watch our wing-tip closely and fly an egg-shaped loop for illustration. As we pull back on the stick to initiate the maneuver we see the wing-tip arcing upward just above the horizon and coming to the vertical position. Just past vertical the motion of the wing tip relative to the horizon seems to stop. A moment later it seems to speed up, change direction, and then stop again. Just past vertical on the downside of the maneuver we detect the arcing motion of the wing-tip again relative to the horizon which increases and then stops as we pull to level flight.

To learn to fly a perfect loop we begin with wings level and a constant heading then focus our attention to the wing-tip and a distant reference point such as a hill or bluff. We then inscribe a circle on the reference point.

This is much easier to do in a high-powered aerobatic aircraft with a favorable horse-power to weight ratio. The powerful engine pulls the light plane around the set arc of the loop with little difficulty. If horse-power is a bit lacking, the pilot must exercise more finesse on the stick pressures and movement.

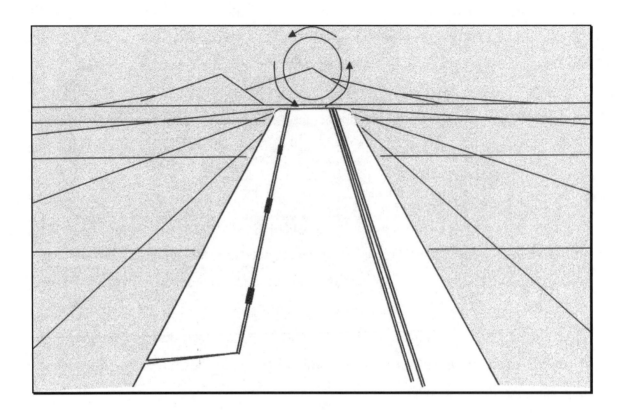

4-6 At level flight, the pilot observes his left wing-tip on or just below the horizon and begins the loop. The first thirty degrees of rotation sets the length of the radius and defines the size of the circle. The wing-tip inscribes equidistant portions around the circumference. By watching this movement, the pilot is aided in determining the amount of stick pressure to apply to make the loop round in appearance. The stick must be pulled and held straight back (not to the right or left) to avoid heading changes as the loop is flown.

Sound

Every aircraft is distinctive, unique, recognizable, and predictable in its performance apart from any other aircraft, even of the same make and model. Often the sound of an aircraft alone will distinguish it.

 We listen carefully to our engines (and propellers) at start-up, run-up, take off, cruise, when landing and everything in between. In other words, we are constantly listening, assessing, and making control adjustments. If something does not sound just right we are the first to know, or should be.

When the engine and propeller, in level flight, are subjected to a load as when the angle of attack is changed, the sound of the engine and propeller also changes. Why, and how can we use this in aerobatics?

Sound waves by their very nature are longitudinal and compressible. Air, the medium in which they most often travel, is also compressible. The speed at which sound travels (about 330 meters per second in air) depends on the compressibility, and to an extent the inertia, of the medium. We recognize sounds with a frequency of between approximately 20 and 20,000 vibrations per second as this is the limit of the human ear. Characteristically we recognize a particular sound by its overtones and quality such as distinguishing a violin from a trumpet or by a sounds pitch which also allows us to determine whether a sound is moving towards or away from us. Sounds are described as soft or loud as a measure of their intensity.

Propellers can be thought of as small airfoils, with a twist, rotating in a geometric plane, which is actually perpendicular to the path of flight, yet develops thrust (lift) in the forward direction.

The propeller blade has a twist to it which is most pronounced at the hub and less so at the tip. The purpose of the twist is to keep the angle of attack along the blade the same from hub to tip and thus improve efficiency.

To further improve efficiency at various flight speeds and engine power settings, hubs which allow the blade to move to variable pitch angles controlled with a governor are utilized. This keeps rotational speed of the propeller constant at a given throttle (power) and propeller (angle of attack) setting.

How does all this relate to engine (and propeller) sounds in aerobatics? Picture this. You are in level flight with the throttle full forward, engine rpms reading 2700, constant speed propeller control full forward, indicated airspeed of 160mph, and you are about to pull back on the stick to initiate a loop.

 Despite ear plugs (you do wear them don't you) and a tight fitting head set the steady drone of the engine is unmistakable. You focus on the low pitched sound. Now you begin the loop with firm but measured back pressure on the stick as the nose of the airplane arcs skyward. Listening intently you notice the low pitched sound of the engine goes momentarily yet discernibly lower. Why?

Obviously, an observer on the ground would hear a distinct lowering in pitch of the sound of the aircraft at the moment it moves away from the observers fixed position. This is the well know Doppler effect where longitudinal sound waves moving toward a fixed observer are heard as a higher frequency and when moving away from the observer are heard as a lower frequency. As for example, when a train passes. Yet, by contrast, a person on the train would hear the sound as a steady fixed frequency.

Why then does the pilot, riding with the aircraft, hear a distinct lowering in pitch of the sound of the airplane with abrupt changes in attitude such as going from horizontal to vertical flight?   To answer this fully we must also consider what happens when a load is placed on a reciprocating piston engine.

First, let's review what we know so far. We know our aircraft is fitted with a constant speed propeller to hold our engine rpms steady at 2700 despite abrupt changes in angle of attack and flight speed. This requires a measurable rotation of the entire propeller blade at the hub as managed by the propeller governor. Just as the wings of the aircraft are placed at a greater angle of attack with respect to the relative wind when we pull back on the stick so also are the propeller blades placed at a greater angle of attack. We also know that sound is a longitudinal wave with many qualities. Sound travels through different mediums at different speeds. The frequency perceived by the listener is affected by the relative movement of both the source of the sound and of the listener.

Let's look closer at an aircraft in level flight through undisturbed air with its engine at full power. For an aircraft in flight the most prominent sound is the exhaust note. A conventional aircraft engine has a four stroke cycle including (1) intake (2) compression (3) power and (4) exhaust. It is the compression stroke that determines the power output of an engine. Compression ratios in aircraft engines are generally between 8 to 1 and 10 to 1 but occasionally are higher. At the full compression stroke the spark plugs ignite the air/fuel mixture and combustion occurs. These explosions inside the engines cylinders are muffled to a degree through the exhaust system.

 It is the air/fuel mixture that when optimal will produce the greatest expansion of ignited gases per compression stroke. When an engine at a given rpm is placed under a load, as when pulling to a vertical line in an aerobatic maneuver, the resultant compensating changes of the engines operations produces a discernible change in the exhaust note.

It is the various and dynamic effects of a reciprocating engine driving a spinning airfoil through a disturbed medium at changeable intensities that produces sound waves of differing qualities and frequencies identifiable to an observer be they at and moving with the source or fixed and at a distance from it. These changing sounds are useful cues in performing any flight maneuver but more so in aerobatics, especially gyroscopic maneuvers where the dynamic effects are pronounced.

Listening to the sounds generated by the aircraft in varying phases of flight are helpful aids to the pilot who must make precise control adjustments as a particular figure is being flown.

Feel

Feel is the subjective portion of the sensation of touch. Touch is the sense we experience when we make contact with an object and discern its qualities. Seated in the tight confines of the cockpit of an aerobatic aircraft the pilot appreciates the sense of touch to an uncomfortable degree with the straps of the parachute and harness pulled tight and secure around hips, upper legs, chest, and shoulders. Mostly ignoring the annoyance of the bindings, attention is turned to assuring there is adequate freedom of movement to manage the aircraft controls and to allow a full range of view through the canopy. With feet properly positioned on the rudder pedals and hand (or both hands) on the stick the pilot feels the movement and resistance of the controls.

To better understand the importance of the pilots feel of the controls, a brief discussion of the neuroanatomy and neurophysiology involved would be helpful. This is important because it is through these mechanisms, coupled with input from other senses, that the pilot lays down memory, develops and modifies learning, and hones skills. That's what practice is all about!

We all possess a central nervous system consisting of the brain and spinal cord and also a peripheral nervous system consisting of the crainial and spinal nerves and there associated ganglia. Nerve cells and nerve fibers connect the systems and run in identifiable tracts or pathways to specific areas.

We are aware of the position and movements of our limbs due to sensory reports from muscles, tendons, ligaments and joints which are carried to portions of the brain and cerebellum by what is referred to as the proprioceptive system.

This system allows us, for example, to know without looking where our hands and feet are in relation to the rest of our body and touch our nose by an outstretched finger with our eyes closed. Not all of the proprioceptive impulses are directed to the conscious level of awareness as a portion of the system is concerned with automatic movement control. We are able to stand and walk and perform other movements without having to think about it.

Details of the specific types of nerves, and their position in the nervous system, is beyond the scope and purpose of this book. It is suffice to say that when the system is damaged, or injured we have difficulty or are unable to perform certain familiar tasks such as recognizing the position of our arm without looking at it. We would also not be able to recognize common objects by touch such as a coin or keys with our eyes closed. We could not feel the vibration of a tuning fork or distinguish two points applied to the skin simultaneously. We would sway when standing…made worse with our eyes closed.

A significant part of the proprioceptive system is the cerebellum. We associate the cerebellum with the ability to maintain balance. This brain structure coordinates and times the action of muscle groups so that our movements are smooth and accurate. Cerebellar dysfunction causes jerking, uncoordinated, tremulous movements.

Looking closer at the sense of touch we are able to distinguish between very light touch such as a tickle and a more pronounced type of touch which conveys the sense of pressure, localization, shape, and position.

We engage the aircraft controls with just enough feel in our hands on the stick and our feet on the rudder pedals to distinguish the subtle feedback coming from the aircrafts surfaces exposed to the outside relative wind.

This feedback travels along the linkage mechanisms of the ailerons, elevator, and rudder and into the stick in our hand and the rudder pedals at our feet. Too tight and tense a grip and our muscles override this feed back information. Our movements become harsh, jerky, deliberate, and we tend to use larger muscle groups such as the upper arm and shoulder when the hand, wrist, and forearm would have been sufficient.

Wrap Up

Flying a simple loop is not so simple to accomplish after all. Though this is often the first aerobatic maneuver a new student is exposed to it is by no means the easiest to do well. Practice alone will not render a satisfactory result. We have discussed the physics of flying a loop and some of the aids a pilot could utilize from within the cockpit. Yet, as with all aerobatics, the defining criteria will be how the figure appears to an observer on the ground. Subtle changes on the controls by the pilot may be necessary to make the figure 'look' round.

This chapter got a bit technical but it serves to point out the dynamics of the exciting sport of aerobatics. Now let's answer our beginning statements.

It could be said the shortest distance between two points is a curved line. If you believe the universe and everything in it curves, as suggested by some scholars, then you could only go from point (a) to point (b) along a curve and the statement is true. The expanses of space are not our concern here but flying curved lines in a loop are. If when attempting to fly a loop we allow the airplane to go off along a tangential straight line, the shape of the figure will distort and our starting and ending point will likely be different. If we pull too tightly at any time to the inside of the circle we may shorten the distance between two points along the circumference but we don't accomplish our goal of flying a perfect figure.

It could also be said a circle is made up of straight lines connected at their ends by the same angle. Looking through the opposite end of the telescope and reducing everything to the smallest of units we see that tiny straight lines of equal length connected by equal angles make up all curves and the statement could be considered true. However, if any of the lines are a different length then the curve does not complete a perfect circle and the statement here becomes false.

The point to be made is this. As with all problems, there is a solution. Flying a perfect loop is no different. It is certainly not necessary to make the problem more complicated than it already is and overwork an approach to a solution by exploring the cosmos for inspiration and the microscopic for clues. We can begin by just looking at the various facets and factors involved and reduce them to short statements. For example, (1) the loop is a circle flown in a vertical geometric plane obeying physical laws, (2) a powered airplane moves in a loop through the medium of air at various speeds and therefore with various pressures on its control surfaces throughout the maneuver, (3) the pilot manages the necessary inputs on the controls based on sensory feedback.

Other statements could be added as needed for clarification but these few are sufficient here. With a basic framework in place that identifies and defines what it is we wish to better understand we begin the learning task. Understanding is based on obtaining knowledge through study. With a bit of digested knowledge we are more likely to be able to determine what is causing a poor outcome and make changes to fix it. Knowing it however is not the same as doing it, which brings us to our next statement.

As with all aerobatic flight it is wise to seek the tutelage of an experienced instructor prior to a first attempt, no matter how many flight hours you may possess or how many ratings you have. Flying the perfect loop...or the perfect mistake...could depend, at least in part, on the pilot determining beforehand if the maneuver can be completed safely. It is unfortunate that loops, or portions thereof, are flown much to close to earth's unforgiving hard surface with devastating results. Safe flying is intelligent flying. Always get adequate instruction before attempting an unknown aerobatic figure, always!

We know for certainty that acquiring a skill takes endless hours of practice. To hone the skill to perfection takes more than just practice...it takes coaching, then more practice, some more coaching, then lots more practice and a continuous expansion of the understanding and appreciation of the task you have set out to conquer. A coach giving instructions from the ground through a hand held radio as he critiques the pilots flying greatly helps the pilot learn the inputs necessary to make the figure look right.

Flying a loop is a lot of fun. Flying a good one will make your whole day. Flying a perfect one will make every moment of your long perseverance worthwhile.

Let's put The Loop and The Roll together in the next chapter and see if we can figure out how to roll the aircraft at the top of a loop and still keep the loop round in appearance. Read on, Oh dauntless aviator.

Chapter 5

Loops with Rolls

LOOPS with ROLLS

Confused...or Coordinated?

5

LOOPS with ROLLS

First Experiences

A circle with a twisty line at the top. That's the image I had in my mind of the figure I was practicing. A 3X5 card clipped to the plastic holder on the control panel of the Extra 230 was directly in front of me. It served as a reminder and a reference. On the card a penciled freehand, grade-school quality drawing of a circle was marked with large letters around the top, "L", "RR", "Ps", "LR", "Pl".

"Clear as mud," I said to myself.

How do I go from inverted to upright and back to inverted at the top of a loop? It seemed more like slight of hand or juggling than flying. Maybe it was all just an illusion performed by a skilled prestidigitator and couldn't really be done. I knew better, that was just a flimsy excuse for my poor performance. It felt like the familiar trying to pat my head and rub my stomach at the same time. Flying the first half of the loop was easy, just pull back on the stick and hold that position to inverted. But what then? Now everything changed. Just rolling the airplane wasn't doing it. It all felt terribly uncoordinated. I tried the maneuver again.

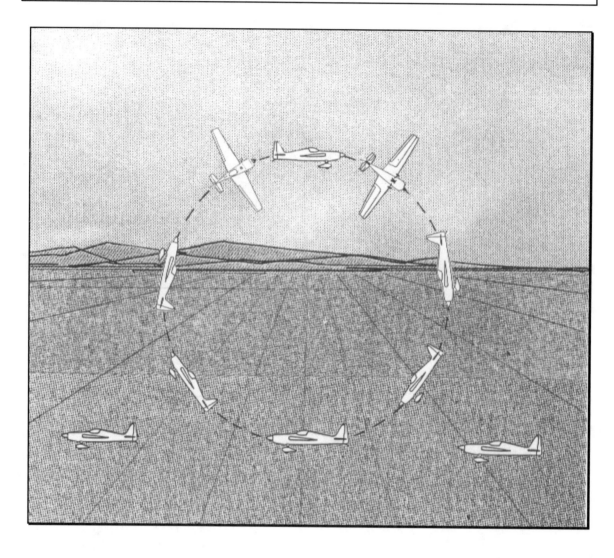

Roll at the top of a Loop. This was the goal.

Repeatedly I drew a flat, rather than an arced line at the top of the loop. Rolling the aircraft upright from inverted at the top was easy, almost a natural thing to do. Rolling again to inverted and pulling back on the stick to complete the loop was a distinctly unnatural feeling. The two halves of the maneuver and what at first seemed to be the equation had been practiced many times.

The first portion, a half loop followed by a half roll, also known as the Immelman, was named after Max Immelman a German pilot of WWI era (Figure 5-1). This maneuver gains altitude and reverses direction, a useful trick in a dogfight in the sky between combatants. The second portion, a half roll followed by a half loop, also reverses direction but looses altitude (Figure 5-2). This is know as the Split-S and if unplanned or entered unintentionally or by accident can be an alarming experience. Diving towards terra firma with increasing airspeed had better have an accompanying plan. Putting the two halve of the equation together seemed to be all that was necessary (Figure 5-3). Yet I needed do something more than just roll the airplane at the top of the loop or there would always be this noticeable flat spot.

Figure 5-1 The Immelman.   Half Loop followed by Half Roll to upright.

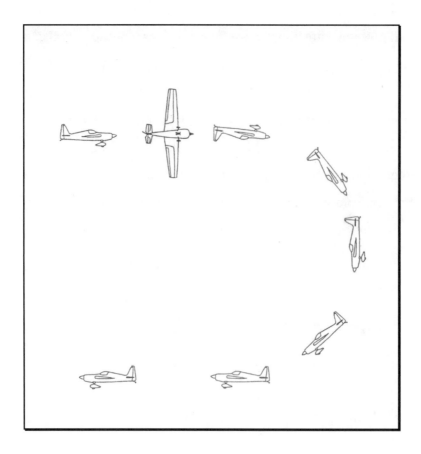

Figure 5-2 The Split-S. Half Roll to inverted followed by Half Loop to upright.

I thought of my first experiences learning how to roll the aircraft. Back then it was hard enough just trying to keep the nose from dropping as the plane rolled to knife-edge and on to inverted. And we were starting from upright. Now I would be rolling the aircraft starting from the inverted position. Some how, that just felt uncoordinated. Like switch hitting or batting from the left rather than the right.

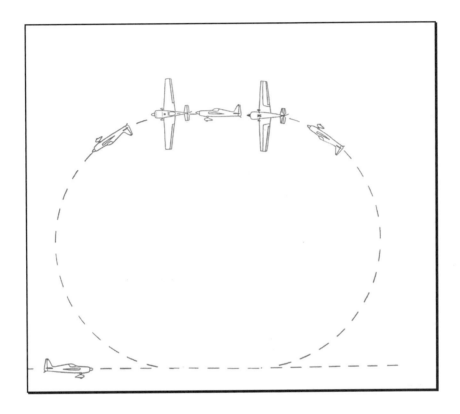

Figure 5-3 Half Loop and Half Roll followed by Half Roll and Half Loop. The top of this figure is distinctly flat and would be down-graded in an aerobatic contest.

The trick back then was to manage the rudder precisely. It was necessary to know when the aircraft was exactly at knife-edge and apply the proper amount of rudder to keep the nose where it needed to be. For a roll from straight and level flight, that meant keeping the nose above the horizon. Now, as the aircraft arced over the top of the loop, the view of the horizon would be changing if the shape of the loop was to be maintained.

I looked back at the drawing on the 3X5 card and mentally deciphered the inscription. "L" meant roll Left, "RR" meant Right Rudder, "Ps" push, "LR" Left Rudder, "Pl" Pull. Hmm…same movements for a horizontal roll from upright.

I still couldn't get this reversal effect of starting the roll from inverted out of my head. It was like looking at a photograph negative and trying to figure out what the finished picture would look like.

I circled around the practice area a couple of times enjoying the desert vistas of southern Utah and near by St. George, where we had made our new home. In the distance to the east were the towering white columns of Zion's National Park.

The few clouds in the area seemed to nestle around and over the tallest peaks. The summer sky was otherwise clear inviting a sight seeing flight rather than aerobatics. As if by inspiration from the beauty of the surroundings it suddenly dawned on me what I was doing wrong.

That's it! The roll needs to be curved and centered along the circumference at the apogee of the circle, not just flown straight over the top. It needs to start before reaching the top of the circle. But by how much?

Picturing the number of degrees in a circle I figured the starting point of the first half roll should be roughly 160 degrees. Then upright exactly at the top or 180 degrees, and roll to inverted by about 200 degrees for the second half roll to continue the loop (Figure 5-4). A vertical compass would be a neat gimmick I thought but then the fast action of the roll wouldn't give me enough time to look at it anyway. I was just going to have to time the roll somehow by what I could reference by looking out of the cockpit. The cockpit view would be continuously changing. I needed to envision what these changes would be.

It wasn't just a half loop followed by a half roll and then immediately a half roll followed by a half loop. The half roll needed to be complete at the apogee, not started there! I had been waiting to long to begin the roll. So long in fact I could sense the top of the loop was flat. I had needed to pull the nose down and back onto the arc of the loop after completion of the roll. I should have already been on the arc. I was also needing to apply rudder and sometimes aileron to stay on heading.

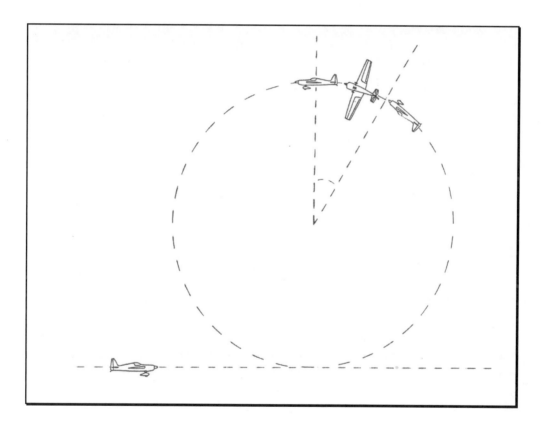

Figure 5-4 The Roll needs to be initiated about 20 degrees from the apogee of the Loop.

"These loops and rolls must look awful from the ground," I said to myself hoping there was not a critical eye watching below, but knowing there always is. I tried a few more, with some improvement, then called it a day and headed back to the airport

Reflections

With the airplane back on the ground and safely secured in the hangar I removed the 3X5 card from the control panel. It's not just a circle with a twisty line at the top, it is a whole lot more involved than that I realized.

I had the correct basic idea. I even had the correct control placement necessary to pull off the maneuver. What I did not have was the precise timing, amount of control input needed, and situational awareness necessary to make the maneuver look good.

Skillfully flown this is a very beautiful and graceful figure. Generally, the pilot senses if the roll at the top is turning out as planned when the loop and roll blend harmoniously. To accomplish that, several critical and perfectly timed actions are required.

As with all aerobatic figures we begin from straight and level flight, wings equidistant on the horizon. If the wings are not level the, loop portion of the figure will be distorted and off heading. As we pull back on the stick to set the arc of the loop, though the engine is at full power, we will decelerate because of gravity's effects. Recall our discussion of gyroscopics, torque, and "P" factor in chapter 1. These forces are ever-present and experienced most when the aircraft is slow, as at the top of a vertical figure such as a hammerhead, loop, etc. and the engine is at full power. They are managed with rudder and aileron as necessary to maintain heading. They may have an effect on the amount of rudder and stick pressures needed for the rolling portion of the figure and the return to the looping portion.

For discussion, let's break the roll at the top of the loop into sections and look at each one carefully.

First, we will examine the beginning of the roll. This is at or about 160 degrees from the horizontal starting point depending on how quickly the roll can be accomplished. The pilot is almost inverted and watching for the horizon to appear towards the bottom of the field of vision. At this point there is seen mostly sky and some earth. Left stick is applied to initiate and maintain the rolling action.

The next step is where coordination or confusion enters the formula. Approaching knife-edge flight at the quarter roll position, the pilot blends in Right (down) rudder pressure to pull the nose of the aircraft onto the arc of the loop. If top (left) rudder is depressed the aircraft flies a tangential line off the circle (Figure 5-5). If no rudder is used the aircraft flies a noticeable segmented line. Too much rudder and the aircraft drops below the arc of the circle.

The roll rate, and the point on the circle where the roll is started are critical. Starting the roll to early skews the shape of the figure and distorts the symmetry of the loop and roll. It is, for example, like squeezing or pulling a balloon out of shape. The effect on the symmetry of the figure would be similarly distorted should the roll be initiated to late. Aircraft with very fast roll rates will easily complete the roll even if started near the top of the loop. Still, however, unless some effort is made to manage the rudders there will be a discernable distortion at the top.

Next, as the roll continues from knife edge to upright flight the pilot is steadily blending out Right rudder and blending in Forward stick. A pause at the completion of the half roll is natural. Aerobatic figures end with the aircraft returning to level flight. The problem here is the figure is not yet over. In fact, the pilot is near but not-quit at the top of the loop, almost but not-yet upright, and still rolling at a constant rate. Planned perfectly, the aircraft will traverse the apogee in the upright position and continue the roll with out hesitation. The pilot's input on the controls are very subtle, not harsh or deliberate, pressures more than distinct movements. Almost slight-of-hand…and feet.

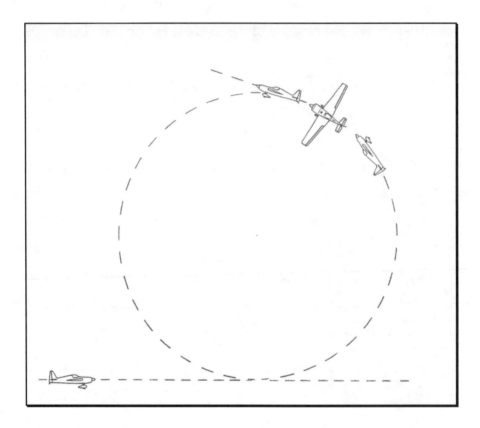

Figure 5-5 Pressing the top rudder at this point will cause the aircraft to fly a tangential line to the circle and distort the shape of the loop.

Now, the aircraft must continue to roll as the top of the loop is traversed. The pilot must keep the shape of the loop symmetrical. This is much easier said than done. The temptation is to just roll and pull. Much like performing the split-S and just forget all this blending hocus-pocus. However if everything has not been managed well up to now the pilot will likely be off the arc of the loop. Efforts to save the figure simply distort its shape. Squeezing the balloon will not make it round. Sometimes finesse and skill will make mistakes less obvious to a critical eye on the ground, but don't count on it.

Assuming all has gone as planned, up to this point, the pilot now blends out Forward stick pressures while blending in Left (down) rudder through the knife-edge position. Remember the down rudder is the one towards the inside of the loop. Airspeed is building on the backside of the loop as the aircraft descends. The amount and duration of rudder input will be proportionally different compared to the front side of the loop where the aircraft was ascending and air speed was diminishing.

Recall that the stick had been moved and held to the left to initiate and maintain the roll. This input must now be removed to stop the rolling action, at about 200 degrees in our example. The pilot should be on the arc and flying the backside of the loop. If the roll is stopped to early or to late the aircraft will be off heading at the completion of the loop and the wings will not be level with the horizon.

The completed roll should have been centered over the top of the loop.

Wrap Up

The whole experience of my first attempts, learning to fly a roll at the top of a loop, felt something like hoping on one foot and then another while turning in a circle and pretending to row a boat with one hand all at the same time. It still feels a bit like that.

The continuous change of the speed of the aircraft in a simple loop is difficult enough, add a roll on a curved line and the difficulties multiply. Managing these difficulties well is the challenge of either being coordinated…or confused.

I am envious though appreciate greatly the skill demonstrated by pilots who are able to fly this figure perfectly and even more when multiple rolls are precisely placed as if they were artistically drawn by the aircraft in the sky.

This is a very challenging figure. Combinations generally are.

Next, let's look at something different in chapter 6, yet equally challenging. We'll try flying an airplane…backwards! Can this really be done?

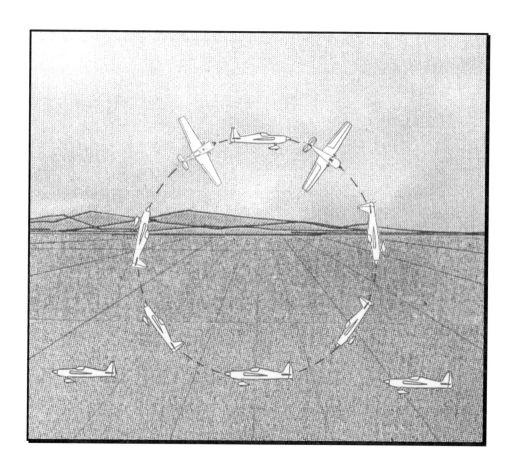

Roll at the top of a Loop. How does the pilot roll the aircraft and still keep the arc of the loop? **Hint**: *Review the chapter on Rolls. Right rudder, Push, Left rudder, Pull...still applies if the pilot rolls Left at the top of the loop. Why? Because, at the beginning of the roll, near the top of the loop, the pilot is inverted. At a quarter roll the down (Right) rudder will bring the nose onto the arc of the loop. At a half roll and at the apogee of the loop the aircraft is now upright. Forward stick Pushes the nose onto the arc. Similarly applying Left rudder at the three-quarter point and then back stick at the completion of the roll will Pull the nose through the remainder of the loop.*

Chapter 6

The Tail Slide

The aircraft ascends on a perfect vertical line and power is reduced to idle...

…it strains to climb higher but is unable. Motionless for just a moment, it slides backwards a short distance then suddenly reverses direction.

THE TAILSLIDE

Poised motionless and silent at the top of a perfect vertical line the tiny red white and blue airplane appears for a brief moment as if it were a painted speck on a blue canvas sky. Its rigid wings have carried it as high as possible against nature's forces.

It strains like an out stretched arm wishing to go further, but unable, against gravities pull. For just that moment, but no longer, physical laws seem to retreat, as if allowing an added heart beat of time for observance.

Reluctantly, slowly, the brightly colored craft gives way to earth's demands and begins a reverent, respectful, backward withdrawal. Poised like a ballerina it bows low, then with a graceful swing reverses direction. Beautiful! Unforgettable! Inspiring!

6

THE TAILSLIDE

First Experiences

Airplanes were never designed, or intended, to fly backwards! That's just logical isn't it? They are built to fly forward in a simple understandable way. The ridged wings of airplanes have a curved leading edge to meet the relative wind and a thin squared off trailing edge where hinged ailerons are attached. At the tail there is a ridged vertical stabilizer behind which, the hinged rudder is attached. Behind the tail's ridged horizontal stabilizer are the hinged elevators (Figure 6-1).

6-1 Extra 230. Rudder controls yaw, elevator controls pitch, aileron controls roll.   In this picture, the pilot is holding full left rudder, full forward and full left stick.

Rigid surfaces towards the front meet the wind, then movable surfaces behind to control the aircraft. Ingenious!

The control cables, bell cranks, push rods and other apparatus connecting the movable surfaces to the rudder pedals on the floor and the stick in your lap need only be strong enough to withstand deflection into the relative wind for directional control.

Otherwise, they remain for the most part neutral. Trailing behind the ridged surfaces, they have no need to carry the main load. That's what the rigid surfaces do.

Suppose we were to reverse all this, and put the hinged parts in front and the ridged parts behind. We would need extremely strong hinges, push rods, cables, stops, and all to keep the movable parts from being torn away and the pilot would need all the strength that could be mustered just to hold the controls in the position wanted. Flying the aircraft would be like carrying a door in the wind. If the thin edge of the door could be held directly into the wind then all would be well. If however the wind caught the flat side of the door................well, you get the idea.

Picture now an airplane out of energy at the top of a vertical line and moving backwards. There really is no control. All the pilot can do is brace the stick and rudders as tightly as possible to avoid sudden hard movements or damage to the plane and hang on until the weight of the engine swings the nose earthward and air moves across the wings and tail in the proper direction. How can such a wrestling match in the cockpit between pilot and airplane look so graceful, almost gentle to spectators on the ground? Planning!

Aerobatic aircraft generally have large rudders and substantial elevators. With the aircraft moving in the forward direction, these prominent rearward movable surfaces allow great directional control and authority. The pilot can briskly move the rudder and or the elevators, (and therefore the tail of the aircraft) to execute particular maneuvers.

As such, these large flat surfaces are the first to catch the wind should the aircraft ever begin to move backwards. When the rudder and elevators move..........and you didn't move them..........the forceful, sudden, and demanding surprise brings a respectful awakening.

Such a surprise is forever waiting to pounce like a hungry tiger on the unwary inattentive aerobatic pilot. Not that your humble servant penning these lines might have been such a pilot…vanquish the thought….but I have heard others who tell nearly believable tales of just such experiences.

One such story begins on a soft summer day with pleasing warm temperatures inviting one to dishabille as socially acceptable and enjoy the suns rays. From off the airports dark heat absorbing roads and tarmacs, one could see rising wavy columns of air distorting background images of walkways and buildings. The air-thinning heat would cause an airplanes takeoff roll to be extended. Increased speed would be needed for liftoff. Performance and climb rate would also suffer from the stifling heat.

A few of us good-old-boys were just sitting around the local FBO, talking about the density altitude and such and exchanging stories, mostly true, of things we'd done (or wished we'd done), and adding more than a bit of sauce to make it all palatable. Every now-and-then we would comment on a particular pilots landing (always the bad ones as this somehow made us feel we could have done better). We would occasionally notice the long take off roll of the cargo carriers, wondering how they got off the ground at all so heavy laden on such a warm day.

Now amongst this group of incorrigible 'want-to-be' was a past middle age pilot extraordinaire who claimed to have flown everything imaginable and with skill and flare to put us all to shame. He described sleek military jets flown when Uncle Sam employed him to protect us all, and on down to the wood and fabric home-built he assembled in his garage in record time.

Intrigued by his stories I asked if he had flown any aerobatics.

"Of course! What do you want to know about aerobatics?" He answered in a confident and self-assured tone.

"Well I was just wondering how your little homebuilt handled tail-slides, you see I was out trying some this morning and...."

"Tail-slides," he interrupted. "Easiest thing in the world, just fly straight up, cut the power and hang on 'til she flips around on you."

"Yes but what about the slide its self, you know the part where the plane is moving back wards, how do you fly that part?" I questioned.

The pause before his response seemed uncharacteristic. "You can't *fly* a plane backwards." He answered with a look of bewilderment. Readjusting the baseball style cap shading the white of his scalp and short hair he leaned his thin frame forward a bit and smiled with an accompanying wink. "That would be quite a trick now wouldn't it?"

"Actually it would," I answered. "But when I was up flying this morning I found that...."

Just then the noise of a passing jet on takeoff muffled my response. Before I could continue, others in the group had made comments of the novelty of an airplane that could fly backwards and what a great air show routine it would be. After the laughter subsided a bit I attempted to continue.

"I was trying some tail-slides and ....well what do you call it if you're flying the aircraft and it is going backwards?"

"Scared sh--less," was an obscure response some place in the playful group along with more laughter.

With this unruly bunch off on a tangent (and more comments about body functioning embarrassments and cleanup in such situations), it seemed my point would not be taken seriously at all.

"Airplanes can go backwards they just don't fly backwards." Our guru of sorts continued. "You're right in a sense, and I know what you mean, I've been there and it can be scary .... an airplane standing on end falling out of the sky.......that's pretty scary."

"So what did you do?" I questioned, half fearing more comments from the irreverent bunch and knowing I had now really stepped into it up to my ankles.

"It's more what I didn't do...and wished I had."

Without the need for an additional question he continued.   "It was scary, the stick was jerked clean out of my hand and banged around like a loose bolt in a tin can. Before I could get hold of the stick the rudder pedals jumped like there was a jackhammer under them. Everything was jerking around so hard I thought the ailerons and the tail of the airplane was gone for sure. Should have held the controls tight...real tight."

"Then what happened?" A voice questioned from amongst the now attentive listeners.

"Well it was like riding the orneriest bull there is in a county rodeo and trying to decide which would hurt most, staying on or getting thrown off."

"So then what did you do?" I asked again, knowing his story was building steam and certainly not yet over.

"It's what the airplane did, why it swapped ends and turned around faster than a spring in a trap. I flung around with it as if I were at the end of a thirty-foot whip! Next thing I know I'm looking straight down at the ground with trees so close I could see squirrels eating nuts."

The continuous expanding smile on his rustic sunburned face curled his cheeks, eyes, and forehead lifting the already loosened baseball cap. He was really enjoying telling this story. Somehow, I knew it wasn't the first time he had had such an attentive audience. The gentle morning breeze reminded me there was increasing hot air blowing around our little group, yet this old pilot seemed to be making a point.

He continued with out taking a breath. "I yanked back on the stick and held on to it so tight you would have thought rigor-mortise had set in. There I was stiff and frozen as a Thanksgiving turkey and thinking I'd soon be cooked... and then I saw it!"

"Saw what?" Some one from the group had really taken the bait.

"The airport of course, I landed and went home."

The laughter from everyone within earshot was uncontained and continuous for several seconds. He looked my way with an assuring wink and gestured again as if he was still holding tightly to the aircrafts controls.

With that our little fat-chewing session ended, the group disbursed, and each member set off supposedly to pursue more purposeful endeavors. I returned to my hangar to view, and examine again, the rudder of my plane just at the level of the elevator. Hold on tight...real tight, was my only thought.

Reflections

The tail-slide, as the name implies, is a maneuver in which the aircraft is positioned on a vertical climbing line and the engine power is brought back to idle. The plane then coasts upward on the line until it runs completely out of energy. Controls are held firmly to block any potential unwanted movement in them as the plane begins to slide backwards. The controls are then quickly placed in the position needed to assure the slides direction. The plane *slides* backwards along the now near vertical line about the distance of one or two fuselage lengths and then swings like a pendulum to reverse direction and fly back down the line a distance before pulling out to set up for the next figure (Figure 6-2).

The length of the *slide* and the direction of the pendulum swing is determined by the number of degrees the pilot moves the plane from the vertical line on the way up, often in the last moments before the plane comes to a standstill and begins moving backwards. We really don't want the airplane to slide very far. Remember they can't *fly* backwards and should they be going backwards and picking up speed the risk of damage is compounded. If the pilot has flown a perfect vertical line and the airplane is perfectly balanced the slide backwards could be considerable, even several fuselage lengths. This is much too far for safe operation of the aircraft. We don't want the controls snatched away by the relative wind abruptly moving the flat control surfaces as the plane slides backwards down the vertical line. The rudder could slam into the elevators causing damage to both. Bell cranks and pushrods could be damaged. Control cables could be stretched or even broken. Attach hinges could be bent. Also, the relative wind acts like a brake on the propeller (the engine is at idle and the aircraft is moving backwards) slowing or even stopping the engine. How then is such a precarious situation avoided?

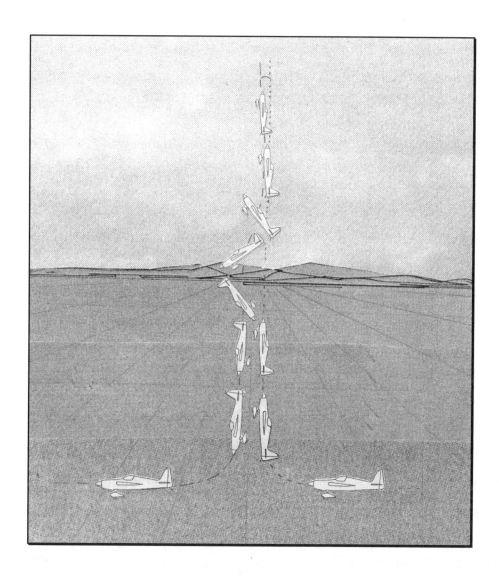

6-2 The aircraft is positioned on the vertical line and power is reduced. Near the top of the line and before the aircraft slides backwards it is caused to lean in the direction of the pendulum swing. A backwards slide of one or two fuselage lengths ensues followed by the pendulum swing and direction reversal.

Anyone learning to fly aerobatics needs to know about tail-slides. It is entirely possible for pilots at some time to find themselves in a nose high attitude and no airspeed. In these situations, taking a firm grip on the controls to keep them from crashing against the stops must be a reflexive action. Let's take a closer look at tail-slides and see what is necessary in the way of planning to keep the maneuver graceful and the aircraft in one piece.

We begin with a pull (or push if inverted) to the vertical line. Actually, this is a quarter of a loop (Figure 6-3 and 6-4). Even though the aircraft may be aligned with the vertical, there still remains some horizontal movement. Recall from our discussion of loops that an object moving in a circle, or in this case portion of a circle, has continuously changing values of acceleration and velocity vectors. We are unable to change directly from horizontal acceleration to vertical acceleration. Any remaining horizontal movement at the top of the vertical line may effect the direction of the pendulum swing after the slide, as we will see in a moment.

As the vertical line becomes well established and we begin to ascend, the throttled is reduced to idle. The airplane slows and the effectiveness of the controls diminishes. We find ourselves greatly anticipating just when the airplane will run out of energy and start sliding backwards. We know we have to determine this moment exactly.

But how? The airspeed indicator does not have negative numbers on it. It wouldn't be of much help anyway as it is poorly effective at low speeds even going forward. We know that when the airspeed bleeds down past minimum figures though, the tail-slide is about to happen.

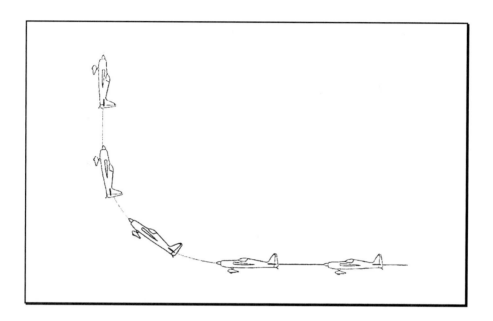

6-3 The pilot feels he has flown this line to reach the vertical, however.........

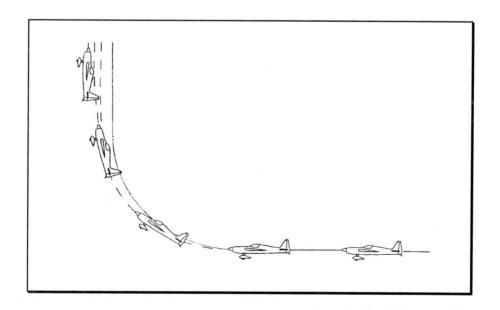

6-4 ...some horizontal acceleration continues on the line.

We also know we actually don't want to be perfectly vertical when we reach the top of the vertical line. A short slide, one or two fuselage lengths will be adequate. We would also like to make the choice as to whether the pendulum swing after the slide will be forward or backwards. If we remain perfectly vertical the airplane may slide a considerable distance and make the choice of the pendulum direction for us.

So what do we do?

To avert damage to the plane from a long accelerated slide and to make sure we pitch down in the direction we desire there are at least three things we must do.

The first is to make use of the least expensive piece of equipment on our airplane...a piece of heavy string about six inches long! This we have attached to the sighting device so that it trails back like a flag in a stiff breeze when the aircraft is in flight and hangs limp otherwise. This technological marvel is our zero-speed indicator. After we have set the vertical line and have kept the wings equidistant and fixed on the horizon by managing any adverse torque or gyroscopics (there may still be some even though we have reduced power) we watch the piece of string intently. When it begins to slump we are almost at the top of the vertical line. The tail slide will happen within the next couple of seconds.

We have decided we want the aircraft to pitch forward after the slide. In this case we will be upright as the nose of the aircraft falls forward and down, going past vertical and back again as if it were a clapper of a bell. To make sure this happens the second thing we must do is pitch in the direction wanted. The airplane must be made to lean forward just enough that the weight of the engine is forward of the center of gravity. Like balancing a broom by the tip of its handle on your finger and allowing the broom to fall to one side or the other.

We are rapidly running out of forward airspeed and therefore control of the aircraft. Should the tail-slide start before we are ready the outcome may be unpredictable. As the string slumps, we move the control stick slightly forward. This places the aircraft off the vertical line by just a few degrees yet enough to assure we pitch forward.

Still intently watching the string, we prepare for the next fraction of a second. The string suddenly reverses direction. We are going backwards! Now what?

Airplanes can't *fly* backwards. But we are going backwards and must still control the aircraft. Everything is in reverse now. We want the nose to fall forward so the third thing we must do in this case is to pull *back* on the stick and hold it very securely. Because we don't want the rudder to swing to one side or the other as we slide backwards we jam our feet tightly on the pedals to block any movement. Holding tightly to the stick and pressing firmly on both rudder pedals we hang on. Within just a moment the nose of the aircraft falls through the horizon then swings once like a pendulum and heads straight down. The string has reversed direction and trails behind the wing. The slide is over!

Time now to bring the power up by advancing the throttle and then, at flying speed, pull out of the dive.

How about we try another tail-slide? This time we want to fall backwards into the pendulum swing. Why would we consider flying inverted on the horizontal line and pushing (as opposed to pulling on the stick from upright) to set the vertical line? Recall that we can't directly exchange horizontal movement and energy for vertical movement and energy. When we are inverted and in this case push to the vertical, we are still moving a portion horizontally as the vector of this direction diminishes. We are looking straight up and going, for the greater part, in this direction but also moving a bit in the direction the top of the canopy is facing (horizontal). Since we want to fall backwards into the pendulum swing, the canopy will be going down and the wheels of the aircraft will be pointing skyward. It is easier to have the aircraft lean in the direction of the horizontal movement (however slight it may remain) at the top of the vertical line, just before the slide. We haven't much time, or energy, or control authority to establish the lean in those last seconds before the slide begins. We want as much going for us as possible before hand. A little wind blowing in the direction we want to lean may also be helpful.

Wrap Up

Tail-slides are impressive aerobatic maneuvers for spectators. They are impressive from a completely different perspective for the pilot flying them.

The old-timer was right. Hold on tight…real tight… is something I'll not forget!

In the next chapter, we will see if we can perform an aerobatic maneuver in about the same amount of time it takes to turn this page. Snap rolls are next.

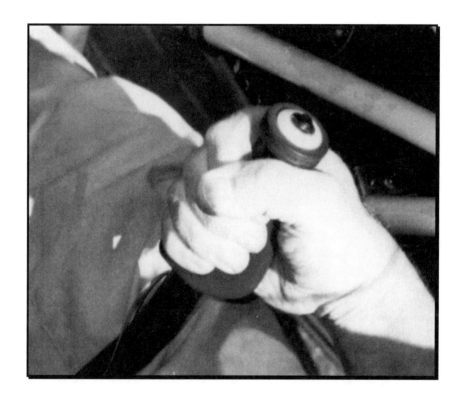

A firm grip to block unwanted movement of the controls in a tail-slide.

Chapter 7

The Snap Roll

Rudder controls yaw.

Elevators control pitch.

Ailerons control roll.

Well……..NOT ALWAYS!

7

THE SNAP ROLL

First Experiences

"Do what with the stick and, I can't believe this, do what with the rudder? You have got to be kidding! Are you sure this is a good idea?" I asked Lewis to repeat the instructions. He suggested we try a Snap Roll before we finished-up the days practice session. I was getting more comfortable with Hammerheads, Slow Rolls and Loops along with the timing and smooth movement of the controls required to perform half-decent figures without major surprises so I felt ready for another challenge.

The explanation was brief.

Momentarily stall the wings with a quick short pull on the stick and in that moment depress full left rudder to cause the aircraft to roll. I wasn't sure I had heard correctly over the background static of the head-set-intercom.

"Push the rudder and the airplane will *roll*?" I repeated with even greater disbelief.

"You've got to be quick and the timing perfect to pull it off but let's give it a try…OK, wings level…… check your speed…… nose up about 15 degrees…….now bring that stick back fast and hit the left rudder pedal hard…………. be aggressive!"

Be aggressive, I thought to myself, right, I'm going to break my airplane in half with these abrupt movements! I had always been taught to be smooth and gentle on the controls. Fly with your fingertips, I had been told. Now I'm about to yank the stick back like it was nailed to a wall and I was jerking it free. The thing will probably just come off in my hand. It just didn't seem like a natural thing to do, neither did stomping on the rudder pedal like I was trying to break a piece of firewood. I was sure I would snap the cable or worse pull the whole rudder clean-off. Then what?

Maybe snap rolls really weren't such a good idea, maybe life's little frustrations could be taken out in a different way like working out on a heavy-bag, or kicking a soccer ball around, something, anything, less potentially destructive. Lewis had always been right before, was he this time?

"Ready…came the voice from the back seat…Go!"

Reluctantly I pulled the stick back and pushed the left rudder. The nose of the Decathlon came up then moved left. The meaning of seat of your pants flying became clear as my weight shifted uncomfortable to the right. The propeller wined noisily in protest like a wounded animal in pain. Despite the restraining straps of the aerobatic-harness I felt momentarily pinned as if flung to the outside of a hard turn.

There was no roll, no snap, just uncontrolled, uncoordinated flight. Surprised and more than a bit anxious I released the pressure on the controls. I was sure I had unpardonably broken something.

"Nice yaw turn." The seemingly unconcerned voice from the back seat commented.

"Thanks….I guess….what happened?"

"Well, you moved the stick like you were shifting truck gears and pushed the rudder pedal like you were stepping in mud."

"Oh….a bit slow?" I tried to sound surprised, but knew my movements on the controls were like frozen molasses.

"A lot slow, let me demonstrate, follow through with me."

The dual controls for both front and back seats in the tandem two-place Decathlon allowed me to observe Lewis' movements. I lightly held the stick and relaxed my feet on the rudders.

"Ready. Now!"

The stick departed my light grip as if Zorro had whipped it out of my hand. At the same moment, the left rudder pedal disappeared under my foot as if snatched away by an unseen force. The airplane seemed to strain for just a split second then suddenly release all pressures with a roll to the left.

"Unload!" Lewis exclaimed and the stick came sharply forward abruptly pushing my hand to the side. Startled I scarcely felt the rudder pedals move under my feet.

With widened eyes I saw sky and earth suddenly change position. Then, as quickly as it began, the blur of rotation stopped and we were upright and flying straight and level...as if nothing had happened. It all took only a second or so.

"OK…your airplane, check your speed and try another one." I was instructed.

Stunned by what had just happened I tried to gather my thoughts together. It just didn't seem possible to make an airplane *roll* by snatching the stick back and stomping on the rudder. It just didn't!

My turn again. This time, I told myself, be lightning quick. Tensely focused I was ready as a compressed spring.

"OK …any time now." Lewis drawled.

Snatch…jerk…nothing. Oh, the rudder! Push….yaw…..slide…..squish. My poor airplane must be protesting such disharmonious abuse I thought. There was No snap, No roll, Just yaw. Good thing we were slow, not much faster than spin entry, something around 65mph or so, now I knew why I needed to check the speed.

"You've got those yaw turns down pretty good, now how about showing me a snap roll? Get your hands and feet coordinated and move very fast. Like you just stepped on an ant bed. Now relax a bit and use your reflexes to make things happen. Set your speed….wings level…..Go!"

I took a deep breath and….Snatch-Stomp…a bit of shudder in the wings…..Wham-Snap…Wow!

"Unload….opposite rudder…neutral stick…not bad." Came some measured praise from the back seat.

We went around about a turn and a quarter or so and off axis before I got things to stop rotating and wobbling.

A few more tries, some more successful than others, and the seemingly aggressive movements of the controls became less intimidating. The old Decathlon seemed to protest less and become more compliant with my commands to jump up and roll over as if I were trying to teach it new tricks.

We landed and completed a rather thorough post-flight inspection. All that jerking and stomping on the controls had me concerned. Everything appeared to be fine. Fabric was tight without distortions or looseness. Bolts and attach points of struts and flying wires were secure. Control surfaces moved normally and hinges were intact. The airplane and I had survived.

Reflections

Thinking about the control movements that caused the snap roll, I stood behind the aircraft and tried to picture what had taken place (Figure 7-1). Lifting the elevator, I could understand that the relative wind would flow over the upward deflected surface and push the tail down causing the nose to rise. The plane would climb.

But the elevator was not gently pulled back as in a climb it was jerked back rapidly. What would that do? And what was this "unload" thing about pushing the elevator forward once the snap started. Why do that? Still holding the elevator up with one hand, I moved the rudder fully to the left with the other hand. Holding the tail surfaces in this manner I thought, great all I have to do now is pull the throttle back and the aircraft will stall and I'll be in an upright spin to the left. A spin…not a roll. How did I get the airplane to roll by pulling the elevator up and pushing the rudder to one side?

7-1 Super Decathlon at rest on the ramp. In flight an abrupt pull back on the stick would pitch the nose of the aircraft up which would increase the angle of attack of the wings and momentarily cause a high speed stall. In that moment, the rudder is aggressively pushed to the stops and the aircraft...rolls!

I knew it had something to do with the speed of the control movements. Performed slowly, as in my first tries, the aircraft wanted to turn and climb, skid and slide, all uncoordinated. Why then, would it suddenly and rapidly roll if the controls were to be moved abruptly?

I looked at the wings thinking about uneven lift and angle of attack and autorotation and such about the vertical spin axis and wondered how all that could be changed to a horizontal axis to get the aircraft to roll. It wasn't making sense. Something would happen when I jerked on the stick that allowed me, in that split second, to push the rudder hard and the aircraft would roll. Did that something have to do with the wings?

I tried to picture the aircraft in a snap roll. There was some pitch up as I yanked hard on the stick and some yaw to the left as I slammed in the rudder…then a rapid roll. The right wing would be chasing itself around the left wing. Why would it do that? Perplexed, puzzled, and deep in thought I moved the Decathlon back into the hangar. Lewis' explanation of stall, then yaw and roll together helped some but I still didn't have a clear picture (Figure 7-2).

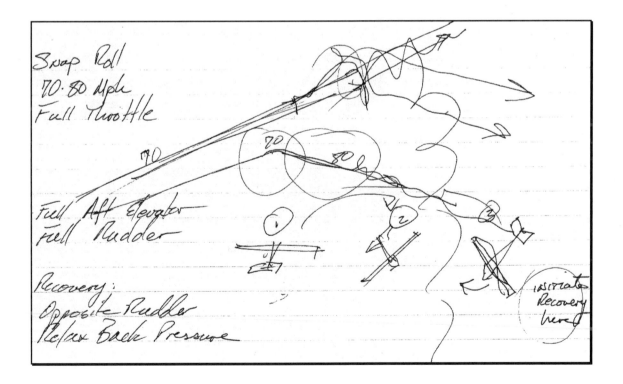

7-2 Initial notes on flying the snap roll.

I sat down to think the whole thing through again.

The left wing would have to be stalled and the right wing partially stalled to allow for such rapid rotation. This situation reminded me of an accelerated spin with one wing stalled more than the other, the engine at full power, rudder held to the stops, and a very fast ride. But in the snap roll we were moving forward, not spinning down.

Yanking back on the stick would disrupt the smooth laminar airflow over the wings...a stall even at high speed. This disruption along with yaw to pull one wing back and advance the other would create uneven and disturbed airflow across the wings. With uneven lift, one wing drops and rotates in a tight arc while the other rises and rotates in a larger arc, and that would cause...a roll!

The axis of the roll would be centered along the slower moving left wing. This would be like taking a toy balsa wood airplane and attaching a heavy wire through the left wing. The wire would be the snap roll axis as opposed to the usual roll axis that passes through the middle of the airplane front to back. In a snap roll initiated with left rudder the airplane rotates around the left wing. If a pencil were to be attached to the tip of the left wing and a pencil to the tip of the right wing different size circles would be inscribed. The left wing's circle would be smaller.

I could picture the snap roll as like instantly creating and then flying through a magical doorway in the sky. The abrupt pull on the stick opens the door wide for just a fraction of a second. With a quick, hard and full stomp on the rudder, and smartly pushing the stick forward, the aircraft passes, just fitting, through the doorway in a lightening fast roll.

It was all starting to make more sense. Stall the wings for a brief moment, yaw-roll in the next moment, rejoin the flight path direction in the next moment and stop the action.

To keep the rotation tight around this horizontal snap roll axis, and therefore increase the rate of rotation of the roll, the stick is moved forward to "unload" drag on the wings.

A quick push on the opposite rudder and the snap roll stops as quickly as it started. This action removes the imbalance in the wings and corrects yaw. Timed just right, the aircraft would be back flying straight and level...as if nothing had happened.

Wrap Up

One-Thousand-and-One. The snap roll takes just a bit longer than the time to say this number out-loud. A well-executed snap roll takes about a second, not more than a heartbeat. That's very fast considering the aircraft must roll 360 degrees to start and stop at exactly the same point. Within that narrow time-frame the pilot must perform five separate but integrated and coordinated movements. Let's consider each of these steps.

Step one. As fast as you would withdraw your hand from a hot stove, the pilot brings the control stick sharply back (but not all the way back) to initiate a positive snap roll. This action momentarily stalls the wings because of the sudden change in the angle of attack and opens a very brief period of time for the pilot to depress the rudder pedal in the desired direction of roll.

Step two. When pitch is seen the rudder pedal is pushed hard. As fast as you would hit the brakes on your car in a panic stop, the pilot fully depresses the rudder pedal. We have counted One.... of One Thousand and One. The aircraft has pitched up, yawed, and now suddenly begins to roll.

Step three. To speed up the rolling action the pilot sharply pushes the control stick forward. We have counted...Thousand... of One Thousand and One.

Step four. To stop the roll the pilot brings the control stick sharply to neutral, while abruptly depressing the opposite rudder pedal. We have counted…. and One…of One Thousand and One.

Step Five. All controls are neutralized, and the pilot continues flight along a given line of trajectory.

The speed of rotation in the snap roll is impressive. The movements of the pilot are quick and fluid, as if one continuous movement.   It's over before you know it.

I could not see what those first attempts looked like from the ground…. though I can well imagine. Learning to fly the snap roll seemed rather like learning to kick box while seated.

To refine techniques and to make sure the aircraft snaps cleanly and crisply, then stops abruptly in the correct position and on heading, takes endless hours of practice. I know, I'm still practicing.

There are many subtleties to learn about the snap roll. Snapping to the left is different from snapping to the right. Positive snap rolls differ from negative snap rolls. Ascending and descending snap rolls differ.   These differences are not only in the performance and handling of the aircraft but in the technique in managing the controls and the abrupt rotations. Our discussion here has just scratched the surface.

Many aerobatic pilots judge the desirability of a given aircraft by how well it snaps. A clean tight rotation with a stone-wall stop is impressive to judges and scores well in a competition. Snap rolls are a joy to fly yet a challenge to perfect.

Each aerobatic aircraft has its 'sweet spot' for snap rolls. At a particular speed the aircraft just seems to start the snap cleanly and then rotates quickly. Only with practice will you be able to find where this spot is.

We'll discuss flying upside-down (inverted) in the next chapter. This is surprisingly difficult when first attempted as you will soon appreciate. Reading this book while standing on your head however, is not required.

Chapter 8

Inverted Flight

Inverted Flight

Things are what they are…even when your view of them changes your perception!

8

INVERTED FLIGHT

The true test of complete trust by another comes when they agree to climb into an aerobatic airplane... with you as the pilot. Now if this trusting, perhaps unwitting, person is a member of your immediate family, some one who knows your faults and short-comings yet is still willing to enter the unknown... well then that's trust indeed.

One such occasion can be vividly recalled. It wasn't long after I had completed initial aerobatic training and practiced my new skills a bit that I wanted to share my excitement with my family. Offering each of them a ride in the back seat of the Decathlon seemed like a great Saturday afternoon outing. Fun they would all enjoy I explained with the usual hand flying gyrations of straight-up straight-down, round-and-round and upside-down. Enthusiasm lacking they looked at me blankly, not even so much as a smile from any of them. Linda declined, as did Lara, Stephen also. Thanks but no thanks they told me. Explanations were short. It would probably make them sick or something worse. Fear!

Of course fear was not a factor, they just did not want to do it now. That left the two youngest sons, David and John. They weren't real sure either, just less inclined to say so, but at least agreed to ride out to the airport with me and think about it. On the way, I told them about how we would be flying inverted and pulling G's and how much they would like it and maybe want to learn to fly and do fun stuff like that. Not a word, just a few head nods and Uh-huh.

We rolled the airplane out of the hangar as I talked about such things as wing loading and control surfaces and airfoils and such. I tried to explain what made the thing fly and why we could turn it upside-down and still keep the engine running. Still no questions, but a few thoughtful, drawn-out…Oh…OK…and more head nodding.

David ventured to be first. In his late teens, athletic, feeling self-assured and willing to try new things he stepped boldly forward. We walked together with purpose up to the aircraft. I helped him on with the parachute and buckled the straps.

"OK just climb in the back and squeeze down in the seat, I'll help you with the restraining harness." I instructed.

Looking around his cramped quarters he noticed the exposed fuselage frame work support tubing at his sides and over head. "Is it OK to hang on to these?" He asked (Figure 8-1).

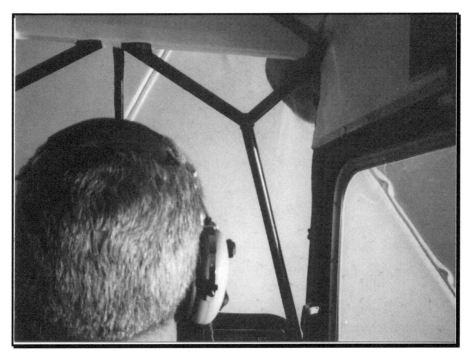

8-1 Holding onto the structural tubing offered some additional security.

"It's OK but you won't need to, the straps will hold you tight enough." I said with and extra firm pull. Demonstrating how to tighten the straps in flight and how to release them in an emergency and egress the plane I stated again. "The straps will keep you in place."

We were ready to go. Airborne we flew out along the shores of the Great Salt Lake to the practice area. David was snug in the back seat bound down securely to the seat and airframe by the harnesses and straps, he could barely move. We made a few steep turns and Pulled a few G's on 45 degree up lines.

"How are you feeling, any airsickness?" I asked over the intercom.

"I'm fine, but these straps feel like they are cutting off my circulation or something." He answered.

"Good!" I said. "Let's turn this thing inverted, look towards the front of the aircraft at Promitory Point."

I knew he would be glad the restraining straps were tight. He had to feel confident in this or rolling inverted would be a totally disconcerting scary event. I also knew what he was about to experience next would surprise, if not confuse him.

The roll to inverted was gentle, almost a non-event. "Still strapped in?" I questioned. He answered in the affirmative with little concern though I could see over my shoulder he was still holding firmly to the structural tubing.

"Hey, did we turn or something, is that Promitory Point out there it looks different?" He questioned.

"It's just like it has always been." I answered and rolled to upright.

David was silent for a few seconds then said. "Do that again!"

I knew he was trying to orient himself to the sensation of being upside-down in an airplane. The sensation is different than almost anything else one can experience. A moment before, while upright, everything looked natural and logical, inverted everything seemed out of place, indistinct, even changed in size and shape.

"OK, let's try something different, this time keep your eye on the lake to your left and keep watching it as we roll." I said and rolled the aircraft Left to inverted. "Which way are you looking now?" I asked.

"Left...no Right...I'm looking to my Right!" David exclaimed with surprise.

"Keep watching." I instructed and rolled Right this time back to our starting point. "Now which way are you looking to see the Lake?" I asked.

"I'm looking Left again...I'm looking to my Left." He answered.

I had purposely rolled the aircraft left towards the lake, which was to our left, so that the canopy would move in that direction as we rolled. Visual contact would be uninterrupted. To keep watching the lake we had to turn our head from the left, then up and around the canopy and then to the right as we arrived at the inverted position. From the inverted position we would now look from right to left as we rolled to the right and back to upright.

"Let's try some other stuff." I said and began a gentle climbing turn to set up for a shallow dive and a low-G loop. A hammerhead followed then a couple of slow rolls.

"How are you feeling?" I asked.

"OK, but maybe we should head back." He answered.

The flight back to the airport and the landing were uneventful. David was still asking questions about inverted flight and why things looked different upside-down as we taxied up to where John, his younger brother, was patiently waiting.

"Well how was it?" John asked in a slow drawl.

What had been near silence between everyone on the ride to the airport, was now a buzz of excitement and exclamations.

"It was great!" David answered. "You won't believe that upside down thing and the rolls and all the other stuff."

"What other stuff?" John asked with an uncertain glance.

I stood back a bit watching and listening with some amusement as the newly initiated and now experienced older brother made explanations with gestures and body language to describe the fun awaiting his younger sibling.

"I don't know about this." John said worriedly shaking his head as we strapped him into the back seat in the usual manner.

"You can hang onto these." David said pointing to the structural tubing.

"Why will I need to do that?" John asked with surprise and more worry.

"You won't." I assured him. Just keep the straps tight, they will hold you fine. With the emergency procedures repeated, I taxied to the runway with my now rather reluctant passenger.

John was quiet and didn't say much on the ride to the practice area, but then he usually is quiet and reserved. Perhaps just some gentle turns and shallow climbing and descending maneuvers would loosen him up a bit from what appeared to be ridged expectation of an uncertain experience. I knew what he was thinking in a way, as fear of the unknown is always the worst kind. Strapped down tight to the frame of an aircraft with a parachute on your back for your first ride in a small single engine airplane is anything but confidence inspiring. I wanted him to enjoy the flight, if that were possible, and experience first hand the effects of G forces and flying upside down. It was supposed to be fun, not frightened until numb. Looking straight down at the ground, from increasing heights as the aircraft climbs, can be unnerving and anxiety producing when experienced for the first time. The bumpy ride and rocking of the plane as the winds picked up was not helping any first time jitters. It was rather like being in a small boat on a stormy sea where the only thought of the occupants is to get to solid ground. Why would anyone want to make everything worse?

"OK John, Let's do some climbing turns and stuff are you ready?" I asked over the intercom.

Silence for more than a few seconds, then a reluctant response. "Ya, OK go for it."

I pulled the stick back gently and made a climbing turn to the left then rolled right in a steep turn back to our original heading. At straight and level flight I asked John how he was feeling. He answered that he thought he was OK, but asked if we were still turning and rolling. The question seemed strange to me at first. Then it dawned on me... he had his eyes closed. To him we might as well be in dense clouds. "Open your eyes John, it is a lot better to try and see were you are going to keep your sense of balance and orientation, just look straight ahead as far as you can see. Pick out a point on the horizon and keep looking at it." I advised him. With that, I rolled the aircraft briefly to inverted then back to level flight. It was over in a couple of seconds. "Are you still with me?" I asked expecting another long pause.

"That was cool!" He said rather spontaneously. "Was that the inverted stuff?"

"Well sort of." I answered. "Check your belts, this next time we will stay inverted a bit longer, keep looking straight ahead as best you can." I added.

John's view directly in front of him was mostly the back of my head but with a bit of neck stretching and head cocking he could see around me to the general forward direction. With this extra effort to see what was going on and watching the distant horizon he was less apt to feel disoriented or ill as earth and sky switch places. It takes only a moment to roll the airplane to the inverted position. The sensation initially is that of suddenly falling to one side and the natural response is to grab on to something to maintain balance. Though securely held by the aerobatic harness, John was understandably holding onto the structural tubing.

"Tell me what you see." I asked.

"Everything looks different, like smaller and less distinct or something, it's weird like I have to tell myself what I'm seeing." John answered with surprise.

We rolled back to level upright flight then dove for speed and tried a vertical half roll followed by a hammerhead. By then John said he had had enough and we headed back to the airport. I had forgotten to bring along an airsick bag. Fortunately, one was not needed.

We landed and taxied up to the hangar where the now assembled remainder of the family was waiting. John mustered a smile to hide some obvious airsickness symptoms as he exited the aircraft with a bit of a wobble in his legs. Stephen, his oldest brother, noticing this could not pass up the opportunity to comment.

"Hey John we're going to Lagoon Amusement Park to ride on the Tilt-a-Whirl do you want to go?" He yelled.

"No, I'll pass." John said in a slow unenthusiastic drawl.

We all chuckled a bit. David and John began comparing experiences of their flight. I put the plane away in the hangar. It had been a good afternoon.

Reflections

With the flight still fresh on my mind I reflected on the experience and sensations of flying upside-down. Why did things seem to look so different hanging from the straps inverted. Nothing really had changed, only the position of observation but that seemed to change the perception.

Flying upside-down evokes a number of unusual sensations. Primary among these is a sense of insecurity the first time you roll to inverted. You know the restraining harness is supposed to keep you in place, but you are not entirely certain, not until you have tested it for yourself. Having confidence you will not be thrown helplessly from your seat as the world whirls and turns around you is an absolute necessity. Without this sense of security the feeling of intimidation will keep you from thinking about anything else.

Wanting to hang on to something is a natural feeling. It is not necessary but the belts need to be very tight and retightened periodically. Before flying any aerobatic maneuvers, and especially any outside maneuvers where excessive negative G's will be encountered, the harness is pulled down very tight initially. After a few warm up steep turns to clear the practice area the aircraft is rolled inverted and pushed up to a 45 degree climbing line. This places pressure on the straps. The aircraft is then rolled upright and pushed to a 45 degree descending line. At the bottom of the line the aircraft is pulled to a 45 degree climbing line. This plants you firmly in your seat. At that instant the belts are pulled tight again. Many aerobatic harnesses have a ratcheting mechanism that can be cranked to tighten them. The belts should be as tight as they will go. After a flight when I release the still tightened belts utilizing the emergency release lever it is impossible to pull hard enough to reattach the harness without first relaxing the tightening mechanism. The straps have been pulled that tight.

With belts secure, the next sensation when inverted is the uncomfortable feeling of blood rushing to your head. That sense of fullness is not particularly painful (unless you are experiencing high negative G's) but does take some getting used to. The physiology of all this is interesting but beyond the scope of this book. Suffice it to say that humans, having become accustomed to being upright, will require a period of acclimation to feel comfortable upside-down.

Now that we are hanging from the straps, we may experience our arms and legs wanting to dangle about. We can hang onto something, like the aircraft controls, with our hands but our feet tend to want to move off the rudder pedals. At first, it takes a conscious effort to hold ones legs and feet in position, later this is done without thinking.

If all this were not enough to contend with, we still have the job of flying the airplane. We need to climb, descend, and turn with skill and fineness...all while inverted. For example to go up we now push forward on the stick (when upright we pulled the stick back). To turn left (which is off our right shoulder), say from a heading of east to a heading of north, we push the right rudder which is on the side of the turn but push the stick to the left which is away from the turn. This may seem a bit confusing, it's not...not really.

Think about it. To execute a simple turn, upright or inverted, we push the rudder on the side of the turn, dip the wing in the direction of the turn, and (for simplicities sake) swing the nose of the aircraft with elevator. We continue to turn until the control inputs are changed. These movements are of course coordinated to smooth out the turn but essentially, they are the ones required. Aircraft can be turned in many ways different than this to be sure but for a simple turn these steps are characteristic. Turns are usually not lead by the rudder however to simplify things and make a point about inverted turns it is helpful to confirm the side to which we will be turning is the same as the rudder we will be pushing.

A turn from a heading of east to a heading of north is a left turn no matter how it is done, upright, inverted, or sideways. What seems confusing is that it is our right shoulder leading the left turn when we are inverted. I have not found it useful to think in terms of opposites when turning inverted. It just seems easier to look in the direction I want to go, point the wing tip there, press the rudder on that side as needed, and push the nose around with forward stick. Let's examine this a bit closer.

A turn to the left when upright is initiated with movement of the stick to the left, which causes the aircraft to roll to the left. The left wing dips down. Now if we were to roll the aircraft rather than just initiate a turn, the left wing would continue its dip earthward all the way to inverted. Now consider the inverted position for a moment. We are still rolling left, however the wing that now dips earthward is the *right* wing as we complete the roll to upright. This same right wing, the one off our right shoulder is the one that dips down if we were just going to do an inverted turn to the left. It dips down the same way it does when we are doing a roll to the left, which we initiated with left stick. We apply rudder as needed on the side of the turn for coordination. In this left banked position either upright or inverted we need to bring in elevator deflection to swing the nose in the direction of the turn. We need top, skyward elevator. Upright we pull back on the stick and the elevator goes up. Inverted we push forward on the stick and the elevator goes… up (skyward). We begin to turn. Simple…isn't it? Well, not yet.

Recall I said when inverted just to look in the direction we want to go and dip the wing in that direction and push rudder on the same side. The surprising difficulty here is not managing the controls but rather deciding which way to turn. As with other decisions when flying aerobatics, we will be 100 percent correct or 100 percent wrong. Why?

It seems that orientation, left, right, up, and down directions and our own position in space relative to everything else has been from an upright position. Any change in this arrangement gives us problems. Even looking in the mirror where left and right appear reversed can seem confusing.

The primary sense used for spatial orientation is vision. Were we to close our eyes and then be whirled about we would be able to appreciate the movement taking place because of the functioning of the vestibular system of the inner ear and other senses of proprioception discussed in chapter 4. We could not however define our exact position in space with out looking, nor could we determine exactly that movement has stopped with out visual feedback.

Vision is the process by which reflected light rays from an object are refracted by the cornea and lens of the eye to form an inverted and reversed image on the retina. The eyes are in continual motion and scan the received images for contrast, shape, and detail. Information from the retina is then transmitted via visual pathways to the vision centers of the brain for interpretation. It is interesting that the eye, like a camera lens, inverts and reverses the images and the brain sorts all this out so we can interpret things as they are and not view the world as upside-down and backwards.

When we change the perspective of vision by viewing the world upside-down as when flying inverted we do not effect the mechanism of sight. The eye and brain still work the same way however the process of the search for clues and details of what the eyes see and the brain then compares to what is previously known for interpretation does change. This process is known as learning. Why do we have to learn to interpret and recognize what we see inverted when we have no difficulty identifying objects and appreciating our environment when upright? Consider this. When we look at a large object at a distance from us, such as a building, we notice its shape actually appears to distort. The portion nearest to us appears largest and the portion the most distant from us comparatively smaller.

The building also rises in our field of vision. An artist depicts the building by drawing converging lines to show distance and a decrease in size as the object rises on the canvas. Light and dark contrasts along the edges of the building emphasize its presence. We know it is a building because our brain recognizes shape and detail including materials, doors, windows, roof, etc. all in there proper position.

When a portion of our environment and objects in it are viewed from a different perspective, such as from an inverted position in an airplane, the visual information, though not changed in substance is changed in presentation. When we look at the landscape while flying upside-down we notice the base of hills and mountains are at the top of our visual field and the peaks are at the bottom. Large objects distort *down* in the visual field to show depth. Many details are missed because they appear out of place as do light and dark contrasts. In short, familiar surroundings just look different...at first anyway. After a period of acclimation, the brain will have two views of the environment for interpretation, one upright and one inverted. Details of this inverted view come more slowly and build on experience and accumulation of time looking at things from the inverted position. Eventually recognition is rapid either upright or inverted.

Once we recognize familiar objects as they appear while inverted we will have a better chance of turning in the correct direction towards them. The sense of reversal of everything, including management of the controls will seem much easier and more logical. Trying to determine which way to turn by attempting to recall left is right and right is left and up is down, I feel, interferes with the natural process of looking were you want to go, recognizing it as the correct direction, and initiating control inputs necessary to make the turn. If you should begin to roll in the wrong direction you will recognize this instantly and make the appropriate correction.

One word of caution, and it is extremely important to remember. While inverted make a conscious effort to keep the nose of the aircraft above the horizon by gentle forward pressure on the stick. This may seem unnatural at first as when flying upright we seldom push the control forward while in straight-and-level flight. While inverted however to forget this and let the nose fall or worse to pull back on the stick invites a thrill ride you may be unprepared for as was discussed in chapter 3. Should excessive descent occur, say in a turn, simply roll upright and reestablish level flight. Be careful not to pull abrupt positive G's though. Excessive time inverted may decrease the ability to withstand the effect of positive G's. The G excursion from say -3 G's to +5 G's is a significant total of 8 G's. You have to build tolerance to these forces. If you should decide to pull through from inverted to upright by performing a split-S, make sure you are slow at the start because you will be going very fast by the time you reach upright.

Wrap Up

Inverted flight when first experienced is a rather disconcerting feeling. The sensation of hanging by the straps and viewing the world from this different and uncomfortable perspective seems to offer few rewards. Fun does not seem to apply and your foremost thought is to get the world back upright...and soon. Once however you feel secure in the cockpit, knowing that you are held firmly in place by the aerobatic harness, the experience begins to take on more excitement. Just looking around, trying to recognize landmarks and ground reference is a challenge. Being able to turn the aircraft with precision and stop directly on desired heading is a bit like learning to fly all over again.

This world of aerobatics offers the ultimate in flying experiences. The challenges to meet, fears to over-come, skills to learn, confidence to build, and thrills to know are like no other. We'll talk more about the various aerobatic figures and combinations required for competition flying and also discuss gyroscopic and tumbling maneuvers often seen in air shows in the next book. Until then, take care and fly safely.

Let's see here…how do I start this thing again?

The Aresti System

Aerobatic figures can be complex, especially in the higher categories of competition. José Luis Aresti of Spain developed a shorthand system to depict the flight of the aircraft and to assign values for difficulty of the maneuver. The system bears his name and is used internationally. Below are the shorthand symbols for the aerobatic figures described in this book.

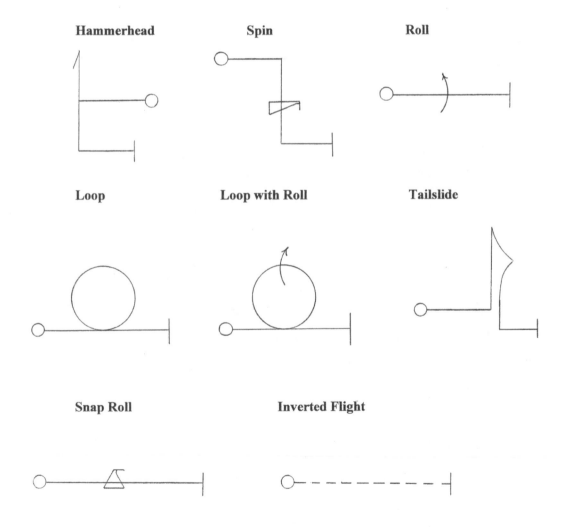

Hammerhead **Spin** **Roll**

Loop **Loop with Roll** **Tailslide**

Snap Roll **Inverted Flight**

The Authors Advanced Free Program

Competition flights include: A Known Program for each category, Primary thru Unlimited, which is published each year in *Sport Aerobatics*. A Free Program which is of the pilots own design and must include certain figures for the category flown. And an Unknown Program handed out at the contest and to be flown, unpracticed, usually the following day.

Figure 1. Pull-Push-Pull Humpty Bump with full roll up and two point roll down.

Figure 2. Sharks Tooth with one and one-half roll on 45 degree line.

Figure 3. Half Loop to inverted.

Figure 4. Inverted Line with two linked full rolls.

Figure 5. Hammerhead with push from inverted to up line and two one-eighth rolls on the down line.

Figure 6. Pull to up line with one-quarter roll up and lay out to inverted.

Figure 7. Inverted one and one-half turn spin.

Figure 8. Pull-Pull-Pull Humpty Bump one-half roll down.

Figure 9. Lay-out Pull-Push-Pull Humpty Bump with one-half roll on ascending 45 degree line and snap roll on descending 45 degree line.

Figure 10. 180 degree rolling circle with two rolls to the inside.

Figure 11. Hammerhead with four point roll down.

Figure 12. Half roll to inverted.

Figure 13. Sharks tooth from inverted with two-point roll on 45 degree line.

Figure 14. Reverse sharks tooth with two one-quarter rolls on 45 degree ascending line.

Figure 15. Pull to vertical with three, two-point rolls up and upright lay out at top.

Free Program in Aresti.   **2004**

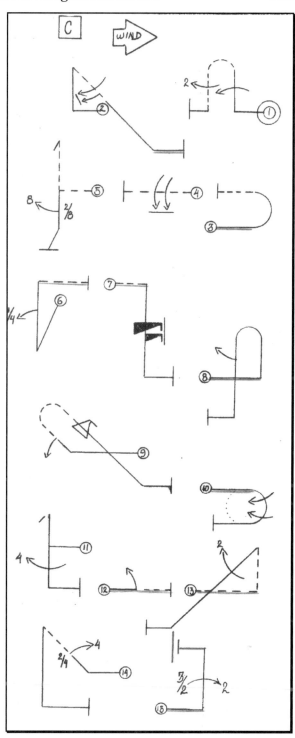

Sidelights

Aerobatics is mostly about pilots and their level of skill and expertise flying complicated figures and maneuvers. Sometimes, however, it is about the aircraft they fly. Occasionally a particular aerobatic aircraft will pass through the hands of several pilots over the years becoming more or less recognizable as the very airplane that so and so flew in air shows or to win this or that contest or championship.

Such is the case of the Super Decathlon N1118E and Extra 230 N444PW featured within these pages. The Decathlon was flown in early competitions and air shows by Patty Wagstaff. Years later the aircraft was restored by a businessman in Ogden, Utah and purchased by myself for the purpose of learning to fly aerobatics. I later sold the Decathlon and eventually moved up to the more competitive Extra 230 which I still own. Patty originally owned and flew this particular Extra 230 to win several national and international competitions in the late 80's. It was later purchased by Damon Wack and flown to win in national and international competition at the Advanced level. The late Janusz Kasperek of Poland borrowed the Extra 230 from Damon and flew to win the gold medal in the Advanced World Aerobatic Competition at Lawrence, Kansas in 1997.

Another Extra 230 featured here is N230GA. This aircraft was flown to win in regional and national competition by Jim Abraham. It was originally owned by Swiss aerobatic champion the late Eric Müller and later brought to the US by Bubba Vidrine. Bubba made several modifications and flew the aircraft to win several regional, national and international contests. It is currently owned by Robbie Gibbs, a competitor at the Advanced level.

There are many great aerobatic aircraft. I have learned, however, that they have no memory. This appears to be certain. Despite easily performing a double vertical snap roll for an accomplished aerobatic champion, it seems that when I am at the controls the aircraft stubbornly refuses even a barley passable figure. I have tried coaxing and coddling to no avail. If anyone out there has a suggestion please let me know.

Chapters Summary

Chapter 1 – The Hammerhead. The Hammerhead was chosen as the introductory figure to be discussed not because it is the easiest, on the contrary it is one of the most difficult, but because it teaches a great deal about aerobatic flight. This maneuver requires the pilot to skillfully manage the aircraft at full power, flying straight up to below stall speed and pivot at the top, then fly straight down. Aerodynamic forces such as gyroscopics, torque, "P" factor, slipstream, and uneven lift on the airplane are continuously changing. A basic understanding and awareness of these and other factors are required if the out come is to be predictable and safe.

Chapter 2 – The Spin. The Spin is a staple figure in aerobatics and is performed to within less than one-eighth of a rotation. One and one-quarter turn spins both upright and inverted are commonly seen in aerobatic competitions and must be performed without the aircraft under-or-over rotating and then must exit on the correct heading. Such precision requires absolute control of the airplane, from the moment of stall that initiates the spin to the exit from the figure when flying speed is regained. A Spin under these circumstances is actually a very docile thing. There are, however, situations in which spins develop inadvertently and unexpectedly in an aerobatic figure or even straight-and-level flight. These can be vicious, frightening, and numbing to the point of inaction or frantic to the point of employing the wrong actions. A deteriorating event now only worsens. The pilot must gain absolute control, and gain it quickly. Spin recovery must become a reflex action.

Chapter 3 – The Roll. The roll requires much more flying skill than first meets the eye. Why? Because this maneuver causes the rudder to become the elevator, and the elevator to become the rudder and the fuselage to become the wing. How you ask? Just picture an aircraft flying on its side. Pulling or pushing the stick doesn't make you go up or down, it makes you go left or right. Pushing a rudder pedal doesn't make you go left or right it makes you go either up, (some if you push the correct one) or down, (and dramatically so if you push the incorrect one). The fuselage is a poor airfoil and cannot maintain lift. How to keep the airplane from falling out of the sky as it rolls requires timing and the correct control movements. How to keep it rolling perfectly on a given trajectory requires endless practice.

Chapter 4 – The Loop. The loop is often the first aerobatic figure an aspiring akro pilot experiences. It is likely though this first attempt was more shaped like the hand written letter "l" than a perfect circle. The physics of the thing just makes flying a perfectly round loop extremely difficult. Angular momentum in a vertical circle against gravity is a complicated concept. Newton had ideas about this when he devised his laws of motion. Equal and opposite forces keep the airplane moving along a given path. Balancing these forces exactly as there vector quantities continually change makes a loop round. Never thought of it in those terms? You don't need to. Many pilots in high powered aircraft fly near perfect loops by just pulling back on the stick and holding it in place with only subtle changes in stick pressure throughout the maneuver. Pilots of lower powered aircraft have more of a challenge.

Chapter 5 – Loops with Rolls. A loop with a roll at the top is a coordination exercise akin to hoping on one foot and then another while turning in a circle and pretending to row a boat with one hand. Well, not exactly, but that is the best way I can describe it. The loop and the roll are difficult enough by them selves. Putting them together in one figure multiplies that difficulty. These are fun figures to fly, unless of course you are in a contest and your ever faux-pas is graded down.

Chapter 6 – The Tail-Slide. Being at the controls of an airplane when it is going *backwards* is a unique experience with its own set of do's and don'ts. The tail-slide, as the name implies, is a situation where the airplane has run out of energy on a vertical climbing line and gravity is pulling it tail-first towards the ground. In aerobatic competition the idea is to have the nose of the plane pendulum-swing a given direction to straight down after about a fuselage length of backwards slide. It is sort of like balancing a broom on your finger…in the wind. Making sure the nose swings thru the desired direction and keeping the airplane from sliding to far backwards are challenges that will make, or break, your day.

Chapter 7 – The Snap Roll. The snap roll is a very fast autorotation that takes about a second, often less, to perform. The movement on the controls must be fast, deliberate and aggressive. This is not the way airplanes are usually flown. Yanking back on the stick (about three times faster than you are thinking right now) and stomping on the rudder pedal to make the airplane *roll* just doesn't seem like a natural thing to do. Stopping the snap roll as abruptly as it started and ending wings level (some times knife-edge) after the correct amount of predetermined roll seems at first close to impossible. This is a very demanding figure and often determines the outcome at an aerobatic competition.

Chapter 8 – Inverted Flight. Inverted flight can be disorienting, even confusing. Familiar objects just look different somehow when you are upside-down. It takes some getting used to and involves some relearning. The idea of up, down, left and right takes on new meaning and seems reversed. The world is the same of course whether viewed upright or inverted. Knowing which control movements will do what while you are hanging from the restraining straps takes some thought.

Postscript

Want to learn more about aerobatics? Contact the IAC which is a division of the EAA.

IAC

International Aerobatic Club

P.O. Box 3086

Oshkosh, WI 54903-3086

Telephone 920-426-6574

Fax 920-426-6560

www.iac.org

EAA

Experimental Aircraft Association

P.O. Box 3157

Milwaukee, WI 53201-3157

Telephone 800-843-3612

Fax 920-426-6761

www.eaa.org

Bibliography

Beggs, Gene. *Spins in the Pitts Special*. Odessa, Texas 2001

Bjork, Lewis. *Piloting for Maximum Performance*. New York. McGraw-Hill 1996

Carson, Annette and Müller, Eric. *Flight Unlimited*. South Africa. The Penrose Press 1994

Cassidy, Alan. *Better Aerobatics*. England. Freestyle Aviation Books 2003

Cole, Duane. *Conquest of lines and Symmetry*. Milwaukee, Wisconsin. Ken Cook Transitional 1970

Cole, Duane. *Roll Around a Point*. Milwaukee, Wisconsin. Ken Cook Company 1976

DeLacerda, Fred. *Surviving Spins*. Iowa State University Press 1989

DeLacerda, Fred. *Peak Performance for Aerobatics*. Iowa State Press 2001

deLapparent, Xavier. *The Aerobatic Four Minute Freestyle*. France. Magic Voltige Publications 1996

Ettinger, Pete. *Precision Aerobatics*. New York. Sports Car Press 1976

Gatz, Authur. *Clinical Neurology and Neurophysiology*. Philidelphia. FA Davis Company.

Kershner, William. *The Basic Aerobatic Manuel*. Ames, Iowa. Iowa State University Press 1996

Langewiesche, Wolfgang. *Stick and Rudder*. New York. McGraw-Hill 1972

Medore, Art Lt.Col. *Primary Aerobatic Flight Training*. Glendale, CA. Aviation Book Company 1978

Norback, Charles. *The Human Nervous System*. New York. McGraw-Hill 1967

O'Dell, Bob. *Aerobatics Today*. New York. St. Martins Press 1980

Robinson, David. *Sky Dancing*. Newcastle, Washington. Aviation Supplies and Academics, Inc. 2000

Smith, Robert T. *Advanced Flight Maneuvers and Aerobatics*. Blue Ridge Summit, PA. Tab Books 1980

Stollberg and Hill. *Physics Fundamentals*. Boston. Houghton Mifflin Company 1965

Stowell, Rich. *Emergency Maneuver Training*. Ventura, CA 1996

Szurovy, Geza and Goulian, Mike. *Basic Aerobatics*. New York. McGraw-Hill 1994

Szurovy, Geza and Goulian, Mike. *Advanced Aerobatics*. New York. McGraw-Hill 1997

Thomas, Bill. *Fly for Fun*.
Thomas, Bill. *Fly for Fun to Win*.

Wagstaff, Patty with Cooper, Ann L. *Fire and Air a Life on the Edge*. Chicago. Chicago Review Press 1997

Williams, Neil. *Aerobatics*. New York. St. Martins Press 1979

The author at a recent aerobatic contest.

About the author

Ed Collins would be the first to admit he is still learning to fly aerobatics. It seems he has always been learning something having obtained two doctorate degrees followed by residency training, specialty board certificates, and a collection of licenses, plaques, and awards.

Flying, especially aerobatics flying, is a passion he enjoys along with sharing his experiences with others. Presently he competes in aerobatics at the Advanced level in an Extra 230 and is a Regional Judge. Other aerobatic aircraft flown have included a Citabria, Super Decathlon, Pitts S2B, Yak 55M, Extra 300L, and Extra 200.

Ed's entertaining way of explaining how he learned to fly aerobatics has delighted and informed many a pilot and non-pilot alike.